Microeconomics as a
Second Language

Microeconomics as a Second Language

Martha L. Olney

WILEY

John Wiley & Sons, Inc.

VICE PRESIDENT & PUBLISHER	George Hoffman
ASSOCIATE PUBLISHER	Judith Joseph
ASSOCIATE EDITOR	Jennifer Conklin
EDITORIAL ASSISTANTS	Sarah Vernon & Emily McGee
EXECUTIVE MARKETING MANAGER	Amy Scholz
PRODUCTION MANGAGER	Dorothy Sinclair
SENIOR PRODUCTION EDITOR	Valerie Vargas
PRODUCTION EDITOR	Patty Donovan
CREATIVE DIRECTOR	Harry Nolan
SENIOR DESIGNER	Kevin Murply

To order books or for customer service please, call 1-800-CALL WILEY (225-5945).

ISBN-978-0-470-43373-7

10 9 8 7 6 5 4 3

To my mother, Ruby Parkinson Olney

About the Author

Martha L. Olney is an award-winning teacher of economics and the author of several economics textbooks. She is the recipient of Distinguished Teaching Awards from the University of California, Berkeley and the University of Massachusetts, Amherst; the Jonathan Hughes Prize for Excellence in Teaching Economic History from the Economic History Association; and was recognized in 2007 by the Stavros Center for Free Enterprise and Economics Education of Florida State University as one of the nation's Great Teachers of Economics. Dr. Olney's previous textbooks include *Macroeconomics*, coauthored with Brad DeLong (McGraw-Hill, 2006), and *Essentials of Economics*, coauthored with Paul Krugman and Robin Wells (Worth, 2007). She currently serves as Adjunct Professor of Economics at the University of California, Berkeley. Her open-access website (http://www.econ.berkeley.edu/~olney) includes course materials for Principles of Economics and other courses.

Preface

Economics is all around us all the time. Much of it is quite intuitive; however, you'd never know it if by some cruel twist of fate you were dropped into the middle of an "Intro to Econ" lecture at your local college or university. That's because the intuition gets lost in the language.

With apologies to *Through the Looking Glass* author Lewis Carroll, whom I paraphrase: Economists use words to mean exactly what we want them to mean. Words like "rational" have a perfectly fine dictionary meaning. Economists use "rational" in a different way, to mean "behavior that is consistent with trying to maximize something." Or, what about "market"? You might think that means a store, a place you go to buy something. Not to an economist. The "market for tomatoes" doesn't exist at your local farmer's market or grocery store. A "market" is an idea, an abstraction, a collection of all the behavior, and potential behavior, of those who want to buy and those who want to sell something.

The key to "getting" economics is to view it as a second language. You need to become conversant in "econ-speak" just as you would in French or Japanese or any other new-to-you language. The ideas of economics are intuitive. The expression of economics is a second language.

ABOUT THIS BOOK

This book is a student study aid in the principles of microeconomics. It is designed as a supplement to your microeconomics textbook. It is not meant to be used as a replacement for the text your instructor has assigned. You will still need to rely on the textbook for examples, applications, and problems.

Microeconomics as a Second Language "cuts to the chase." It zeroes in on the concepts, assumptions, and models that you need to learn. We take a barebones approach here. Our focus is the principles of microeconomics and the language used to express them.

What if you're not currently enrolled in a microeconomics course? This book is a good aid for you, too. Trying to pick up some economics concepts and language? This book will help you out. Trying to follow the news about the economy? This book is for you. Rather than wade through a 700- to 900-page principles textbook, *Microeconomics as a Second Language* gives you the basics to get you up to speed quickly.

ORGANIZATION

Microeconomics as a Second Language is organized in the same order as standard economics textbooks. This organization facilitates its use as a supplementary text.

Economics principles are often expressed with equations and graphs, so Chapter 1 presents the math and graphing tools you need. We dive into economics in Chapter 2, with the model of the production possibilities frontier (PPF), which is about the choices we make in deciding what goods and services will be produced.

In Chapters 3 and 4, the model of demand and supply is presented. Demand and supply is the most often used model in economics. You want to master it. The basics of demand and supply are in Chapter 3, and common extensions are in Chapter 4.

What lies behind demand and supply? The answers are in Chapters 5 and 6. Consumer theory is the basis of demand, and is presented in Chapter 5. The ideas behind the supply curve are presented in Chapter 6.

Some of the material in Chapter 6 applies to any sort of business. Some of it only applies to what economists call "perfectly competitive" firms—small, typically family-owned businesses offering a product that isn't easily distinguished from what is offered by competitors. Chapter 7 considers all other types of firms—what economists call "imperfect competition"—monopolies, oligopolies, and firms characterized by monopolistic competition.

There are times when an unregulated economy fails to produce the amount of output that we—society—deem best. The two primary examples, externalities and public goods, are covered in Chapter 8.

Finally, the Demand and Supply model is applied to what economists call "factor markets"—markets for the factors (or, inputs or resources) that are used to produce output. Labor, land, and capital markets are discussed in Chapter 9.

FEATURES

Each chapter begins with a list of the key terms and concepts, graphs, and equations covered in that chapter. The first use of each concept in the chapter is highlighted in **bold**. The index at the back of the book also contains all of these key terms.

TIP

"TIP" notes in each chapter highlight tricks for remembering concepts or common errors to avoid.

TRY

"TRY" questions give you the chance to test what you've learned. Answers to all "TRY" questions are at the back of the book.

HOW BEST TO LEARN ECONOMICS

Economics is not a novel to be read at the beach. (Though we welcome beach-goers to give this book a try!) Economics is best learned with pencil in hand. Don't just read a new term, write it down. Don't just look at a graph, draw it yourself. Jot notes and questions in the margins. Be actively engaged with what you are reading.

And then comes the key to truly learning econ. Breathe it. Everywhere you look, everything you read, every word you hear—think econ. Think about how you can explain it in the language of economics.

Don't limit yourself in this task to the business news. You'll really "get" economics when you can apply it everywhere. Marriage rates are going down as 20-somethings postpone marriage ... gains from trade explain it. Politicians debate budgets in which prison spending competes with education funding ... the production possibilities frontier explains it. The Joad family in *Grapes of Wrath* is offered only 5 cents for picking peaches ... demand and supply explains it. Despite pollution and climate change, Americans drive and drive and drive ... externalities explain it.

Economics is all around you. To become fully conversant in the language of economics, think econ. All the time. And now, let's begin.

Martha L. Olney
University of California
Berkeley

Acknowledgments

A huge thank you to Judith Joseph of John Wiley and Sons, who believed in this project from the beginning and whose patience with delays associated with my mother's decline is appreciated more than she knows. Thank you also to Sarah Vernon who oversaw the project through production.

In addition, thank you to the reviewers who provided invaluable feedback on this manuscript, in its various stages: Leon J. Battista, Quinnipiac University; Eugenie B. Bietry, Pace University; Lawrence C. Ikwueze, Pace Univeristy; Kathy A. Kelly, University of Texas at Arlington; and Susan K. Laury, Georgia State University.

And, as always, a heartfelt thanks to my partner (now, wife) of 25 years, Esther Hargis, and our son Jimmy K, who gave up evenings with me and Momma's bedtime reading so I could work.

Table of Contents

Chapter 1

Economics Tools: Math and Graphing

Economics studies the behavior of the economy—both the behavior of individuals within the economy and of the economy as a whole. This book highlights the language of economics. It is designed to be a supplement to a standard principles textbook. Mathematical tools used in studying economics are the focus of this chapter.

KEY TERMS AND CONCEPTS

- Microeconomics
- Macroeconomics
- Aggregate
- Positive economics
- Normative economics
- Empirical evidence
- Social science
- Economic models
- Functional notation
- Variables
- Dependent variable
- Independent variable
- Δ means change
- Rate of change
- Two-dimensional graphs
- Horizontal axis
- Vertical axis
- Truncated axis
- Curve
- Slope
- Directly (or, positively) related
- Inversely (or, negatively) related
- Straight line

- Linear curve
- Nonlinear curve
- Convex to the origin
- Concave to the origin
- Move along a curve
- Shift of a curve

INTRODUCTION TO ECONOMICS

Economics is divided into microeconomics and macroeconomics. **Microeconomics** deals with questions about the behavior of individuals: individual people, individual firms, individual markets. Questions in microeconomics include:

- What determines the price of some product?
- How much output will a firm produce?
- What determines the wage rate in a labor market?

Macroeconomics deals with questions about the behavior of groups of people, about the entire economy. Economists sometimes use the phrase **aggregate** to describe any such group. Macroeconomics is usually applied to a national economy such as the United States economy. But the tools of macroeconomics can be applied to any *aggregate* economy: a region, a state, a county, a city. Questions in macroeconomics include:

- What determines the economy's inflation rate?
- What determines the economy's unemployment rate?
- What determines the total income of an economy?

Economic analysis—whether it is microeconomic or macroeconomic analysis—can be divided into two categories: positive economics and normative economics. **Positive economics** answers questions that are usually phrased as "How does this thing affect that thing?": How does a rise in income affect the price of airline tickets? How does a drop in spending by households affect the number of jobs in an economy? **Normative economics** answers questions that are usually phrased as "Should this action be taken?": Should the City Council enact a rent control policy? Should the federal government raise taxes?

Most economic analysis is positive economic analysis. Positive economics requires analysis of a question, but no judgment as to what is best for society. Normative economics requires a value judgment. When offering a normative analysis—*should* this action be taken—it is necessary to state what goal(s) we are trying to achieve. Disagreements among economists are almost always in the realm of normative economics. Disagreeing economists usually agree on the positive analysis: How will the policy affect the economy? But they disagree on the best goal: Is our goal to reduce inequality or to enhance growth? Is it to lower inflation or create jobs? When you hear economists disagree, try to listen for whether their ultimate disagreement is over the goals they hold for society.

The use of **empirical evidence** is also an important part of economics. Empirical evidence means data—statistics, numbers—that can be used to support an argument. How much does spending for macaroni and cheese change when families have less money to spend? "How much" is an empirical question, a question that calls for a numerical (an empirical) answer.

Economics is a **social science** that uses mathematical tools. It is a social science because it deals with the behavior of people. It uses mathematical tools because ideas and theories and models and empirical evidence about people's economic behavior are expressed mathematically.

ECONOMIC MODELS

Economic models are used to answer questions in economics. Economic models are almost never physical models such as a model airplane. Instead, **economic models** are the formal way economists answer questions and tell stories. Economic models are the stories we tell.

Every economic model consists of three things:

- a question
- simplifications of and abstractions from the real world
- assumptions about economic behavior

Change any one of these three things and you have a different model.

For example, if the question is "What determines the price of a pickle?," the model to use is the model of supply and demand (Chapter 3). But if instead the question is "What determines the level of unemployment?," we use a different model. Change the question and it's a different model, a different economic story.

Or, one simplification of the complex world we live in is to divide it into four groups: households, businesses, government, and the rest of the world. When this simplification is made, we are using a macroeconomic model called the Keynesian model (which we'll cover in the companion volume, *Macroeconomics as a Second Language*). But if instead the world was simplified into just two groups—capitalists and workers—then we would be using a different model. Change the simplification and it's a different model, a different economic story.

Or, if we assume that households determine their annual spending by considering how much saving they need to do in order to be able to live comfortably in their retirement years, we are using a model called the life-cycle model. But if instead we assume households determine their annual spending by considering just that year's income, we are using a different model. Change an assumption and it's a different model, a different economic story.

Economic models are expressed in three ways:

- with words
- with mathematical equations
- with graphs

Most models are expressed in two ways (words and one other); some are expressed in all three ways.

   If you don't understand the words, look at the graph. If a graph doesn't make sense, look at the equation or the words. All three ways of expressing a model should reinforce each other. Think of them as three languages all telling you the same thing. Eventually you should understand all three expressions of any model and be able to move back and forth between them.

MATHEMATICAL TOOLS

In a Principles of Economics course, you need to be able to use a few mathematical tools. We cover the most commonly used math tools here. Graphing tools (covered in the next section) are perhaps more important to your success in studying economics. Be sure to refer back to this chapter often until you are comfortable with these math and graphing tools.

Fractions and Decimals

In some parts of economics, we use fractions; in other parts, decimals. You want to be comfortable going back and forth between fractions and decimals. And you want to be comfortable reducing fractions. Examples:

- $\dfrac{30}{40} = \dfrac{3}{4} = 0.75$
- $\dfrac{20}{40} = \dfrac{1}{2} = 0.5$
- $0.6 = \dfrac{6}{10}$, so $\dfrac{1}{0.6} = \dfrac{10}{6} = \dfrac{5}{3}$

Absolute Value

On a few occasions, economists use absolute value. The absolute value of any number is the distance that number is from zero (ignoring whether the number is above or below zero). The absolute value of a number is indicated with two straight lines: | |. So $|4| = 4$ and $|-4| = 4$.

Functional Notation

Much of economics is shorthanded with equations and symbols (or, notation). For example, an economist writes the simple sentence "How many sodas you want to buy depends primarily on the price of soda" as $q_D = f(p)$. Economists say they have expressed the relationship in an equation using **functional notation**. It is important to be able to "read" equations.

   What words are in your head as you read "$q_D = f(p)$"? If you thought "q sub D equals f parentheses p," you'll have a lot of trouble in economics. You're in better shape if you read that equation as "q sub D equals a function of p." But to really *get* economics, you want to read "$q_D = f(p)$" as "quantity demanded depends on price."

Success in reading equations depends on two things:

- being able to translate the functional notation such as f( ) into words
- knowing what the symbols (or, notation) stand for

To know what q_D, p, and more stand for, you must simply memorize their meanings. Memorizing will be easier if you use the same notation every time. Think of it as txting 4 economists.

TIP

Start by making a list of your book's *notation*. Then every time your instructor says "price," write "p" in your notes. Every time she says "quantity," write "q." And so on.

Variables

Economists use the word "variable" over and over. This is one of many times when a commonly used word has a different and more technical meaning in the language of economics than in everyday conversation. A **variable** is something whose value *can* change. The price of a box of tissues at the nearby grocery store may have been the same for the last four months, but economists say price is a variable because its value *can* change. The variable is "price"; the notation we use for the variable "price" is *p*.

There are two types of variables: dependent and independent. The value of a **dependent variable** depends on the values of the **independent variables**. How much a family spends in a month depends on its income. Family spending is a dependent variable whose value depends on the independent variable family income. Family spending and family income are both variables because the values of both *can* change. In any one relationship, there is only *one* dependent variable but no limit to the number of independent variables.

Algebra

In macroeconomics, we often solve algebraic equations with one unknown. For example, what is the value of Y if

$$Y = 100 + 0.6Y$$

To solve this equation, first gather terms (remember Y is the same as $1 \times Y$)

$$Y - 0.6Y = 100$$
$$0.4Y = 100$$

and then divide both sides of the equation in order to isolate Y

$$\frac{0.4Y}{0.4} = \frac{100}{0.4}$$
$$Y = 250$$

Δ Means "Change"

Over and over in economics, we will talk about the change in the value of some variable. Economists use the uppercase Greek letter delta, Δ, to stand for change. So Δx is read as "the change in x." ΔY is "the change in Y." Substituting Δ for "change in" is another shorthand you should start using as you take notes in class.

Calculating Rate of Change

In some cases, we need to calculate a variable's rate of change, or percentage change, between two values. For instance, if Q increases from 50 to 60, at what rate has Q increased?

The general formula for calculating rate of change is

$$\frac{new\ value - old\ value}{old\ value}$$

So when Q increases from 50 to 60, the rate of change is $(60 - 50)/50 = 10/50 = 0.2$, or 20 percent.

TRY

Try your hand at these math problems.
(*Answers for all "TRY" problems are at the back of the book.*)

1. Solve for Y: $Y = 350 + 0.3Y$
2. What is the rate of change of income when income rises from 100 to 110?
3. What is the rate of change of income when income falls from 110 to 100?

GRAPHING

Thumb through any economics principles textbook and you'll see lots of graphs. Comfort in drawing, interpreting, and analyzing graphs is essential when studying econ.

The Basics

Almost every economics graph is a **two-dimensional graph**—a graph that depicts what is happening with just two variables. A two-dimensional graph has a **horizontal axis** and a **vertical axis**. Where the two axes cross is called the "origin." The values of the variable depicted on the horizontal axis range from negative values on the left of the origin to positive values on the right. The values of the variable depicted on the vertical axis range from negative values below the origin to positive values above it.

Any one point on the graph shows simultaneously the values of both variables. Let's make up an example: The variable d is measured on the vertical axis and the variable w is measured on the horizontal axis. Point A in Figure 1.1 represents a negative value of w (it is to the left of the origin) and a negative value of d (it is

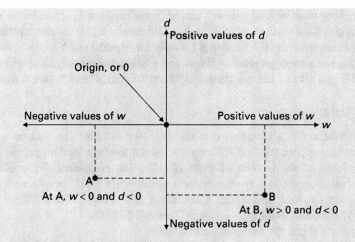

Figure 1.1 A two-dimensional graph.

Two-dimensional graphs depict what is happening with two variables. The horizontal axis and vertical axis cross at the origin. Any point in the graph depicts two values simultaneously. Point A represents a negative value of w ($w < 0$) and a negative value of d ($d < 0$).

below the origin). Point B represents a positive value of w (it is to the right of the origin) and a negative value of d (it is below the origin).

The axes divide the graph into four areas called *quadrants*. Because most variables in economics take on only positive values, we almost always use just the upper right quadrant. So most graphs begin with axes like you see in Figure 1.2.

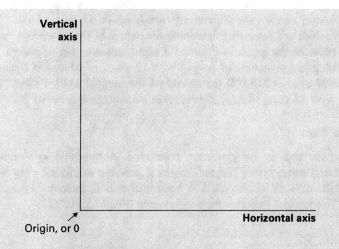

Figure 1.2 The upper right quadrant.

Because most of the variables we measure in economics take on only positive values, most graphs in economics use just the upper right quadrant of a two-dimensional graph.

Borrowing from high school math classes, some books call the horizontal axis the *"x-axis"* and call the vertical axis the *"y-axis."* Be careful if you use that terminology. There are economics variables called X (usually for exports) and Y (usually income), but they are not always graphed on the x- and y-axes, respectively. You will not get confused if you always just use the terms "horizontal axis" and "vertical axis."

Plotting Data

If we have information (data) on two variables, we can plot that data on a graph. For example, suppose we find information on the average income people earned in 2003 sorted by the number of years of education completed. We could write the information down in a (cumbersome!) sentence: In 2003, people with a high school diploma earned, on average, $28,000 per year. People with a college degree earned $51,000, and those with a master's earned $62,000.

Or we could put the information in a table:

Table 1.1   Income Increases with Education

Last degree earned	Years of education	Average annual income in 2003
H.S. diploma	12	$28,000
College diploma	16	$51,000
Master's degree	18	$62,000

Source: U.S. Census Bureau, *Statistical Abstract of the United States: 2006*, Table 217.

It's certainly easier from the table than from the sentence to see that more education means higher income. What about showing the same information in a graph?

To plot the data, put one variable on the horizontal axis and the other on the vertical axis. Often—not always—in economics, the **independent variable** is put on the horizontal axis and the **dependent variable** is on the vertical axis. The independent variables are those that determine the values of the dependent variable.

Each point on the graph in Figure 1.3 represents one pair of values. Point A indicates the average income of people with 12 years of education (measured on the horizontal axis) is $28,000 (measured on the vertical axis). Point C indicates that those with 18 years of education receive an average income of $62,000.

Truncated Axes

Notice that the axes in our graph are **truncated**. A truncated axis omits values between 0 and some value. The two marks // near the origin are what we use to show that the axes are truncated. The horizontal axis is truncated between 0 and 12 years. The vertical axis is truncated between $0 and $20,000.

Curves

Sometimes a relationship is depicted with a **curve** rather than individual points. The curve—an unbroken line that may or may not be straight—may connect actual data. In Figure 1.4, the data from Figure 1.3 are connected with a curve.

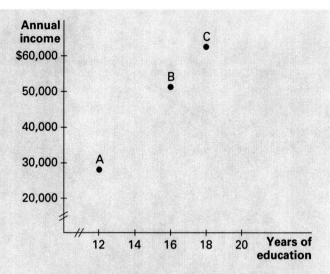

Figure 1.3 Plotting data points.

Each point on the graph represents one pair of values. Annual income is measured on the vertical axis. Years of education are measured on the horizontal axis. Point A indicates that those with 12 years of education earned an average annual income of $28,000.

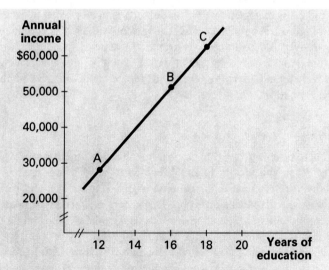

Figure 1.4 Connecting data points with a curve.

A relationship between two variables can be depicted with a curve that connects known data points. Starting from the data in Table 1.1, the curve shows that average annual income increases with years of education.

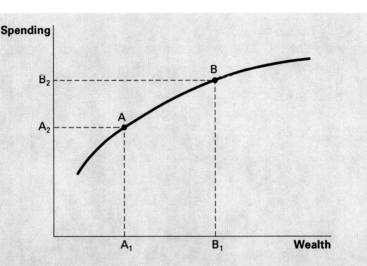

Figure 1.5 Graphs without numbers.

Often in economics we draw graphs without using numerical values of the two variables. If we know that wealthier households spend more than poorer households, we can depict this relationship with a curve. This graph shows that spending increases when wealth increases, but the increases in spending get smaller and smaller as wealth gets larger and larger.

Or the curve may depict a relationship without reflecting any actual data. Figure 1.5 indicates that spending by households is higher when household wealth is higher. In Figure 1.5, a point such as A represents values of spending and wealth. From A, dash over to the vertical axis to find the value of spending and dash down to the horizontal axis to find the level of wealth. Point A represents the combination of wealth level A_1 and spending level A_2. Point B represents the combination of wealth level B_1 and spending level B_2.

Reading Graphs

It is important to be able to "read" a graph as much as it's important to be able to read an equation. When you look at Figure 1.5, what (if any!) words are in your head? One possibility is: "A graph with spending on the vertical axis and wealth on the horizontal axis is a curve that slopes up." This is correct, but doesn't help you much.

Another possibility is "Spending depends on wealth." Again, correct but incomplete. The graph tells you much more than simply that.

A good sentence would be "Spending increases when wealth increases, but the increases in spending get smaller and smaller as wealth gets larger and larger."

Slope

Calculating the actual slope of a straight line or along a curve is sometimes necessary. Most of us learned in high school a formula for calculating slope: "slope equals rise over run" or

$$slope = \frac{rise}{run}$$

That formula works here, too. The rise is the change between two points along the vertical axis. The run is the change between the same two points along the horizontal axis.

Between points A and B in Figure 1.6 the "rise" is $6 - 4 = 2$. The "run" is $3 - 2 = 1$. So the slope between A and B is

$$\frac{rise}{run} = \frac{\Delta y}{\Delta x} = \frac{6 - 4}{3 - 2} = \frac{2}{1} = 2$$

(Δ is the Greek uppercase letter "delta" and means "change.")

Positive or Negative Slope

When the slope is positive as in Figure 1.6, we say the two variables are **directly related** or **positively related** to each other. When the temperature rises (when x increases), more people drink lemonade (y increases). Economists say: Temperature and lemonade consumption are directly related.

When the slope is negative as in Figure 1.7, the two variables are **inversely related** or **negatively related** to each other. When the temperature rises (when

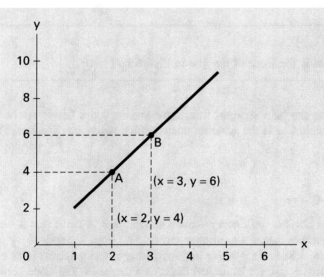

Figure 1.6 Calculating a positive slope.

The slope of a line between any two points is equal to "rise over run." The rise is the change in values along the vertical axis. The run is the change in values along the horizontal axis. Between A and B, the value of y depicted on the vertical axis increases from 4 to 6. The rise equals $\Delta y = 6 - 4 = 2$. Between A and B, the value of x depicted on the horizontal axis increases from 2 to 3. The run equals $\Delta x = 3 - 2 = 1$. The slope between A and B is rise/run = 2/1 = 2.

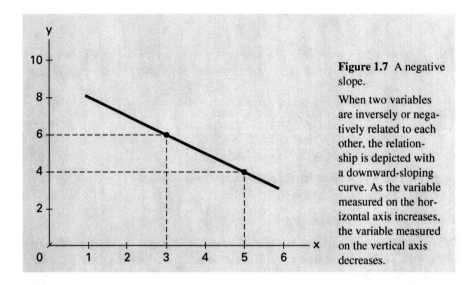

Figure 1.7 A negative slope.

When two variables are inversely or negatively related to each other, the relationship is depicted with a downward-sloping curve. As the variable measured on the horizontal axis increases, the variable measured on the vertical axis decreases.

x increases), fewer people buy wool coats (y decreases). Economists say: Temperature and sales of wool coats are inversely related.

TRY

4. What is the slope of the line in Figure 1.7?

A curve can be a **straight line**, sometimes called a **linear curve**. The slope along a straight line is the same no matter which two points you use. The slope is constant.

Nonlinear Curve

A curve can also be, well, curvy—not a straight line. A curve that is not a straight line is sometimes called a **nonlinear curve**. The slope changes along a nonlinear curve. Figure 1.8a has a positive and increasing slope: y increases as x increases, and the increases in y get larger and larger as x increases. The slope between points C and D is greater than the slope between points A and B.

Figure 1.8b has a positive and decreasing slope: y increases as x increases and the increases in y get smaller and smaller as x increases. The slope between points C and D is smaller than the slope between points A and B.

Figure 1.8c has a negative and increasing (in absolute value) slope: y decreases as x increases, and the decreases in y get larger and larger as x increases. Figure 1.8c is also sometimes called **concave to the origin**. The slope between points C and D is larger (in absolute value) than the slope between points A and B.

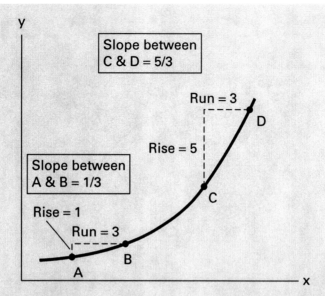

Figure 1.8a Positive and increasing slope.

The slope of this curve is positive—the values of y increase as the values of x increase. The slope increases as we move from left to right along the curve. Between points A and B, the slope is 1/3. Between points C and D, the slope is 5/3.

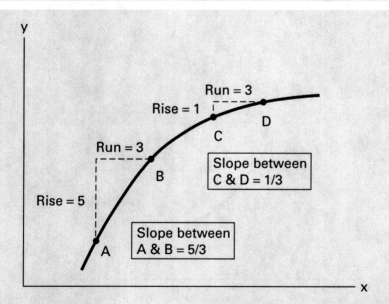

Figure 1.8b Positive and decreasing slope.

The slope of this curve is positive—the values of y increase as the values of x increase. The slope decreases as we move from left to right along the curve. Between points A and B, the slope is 5/3. Between points C and D, the slope is 1/3.

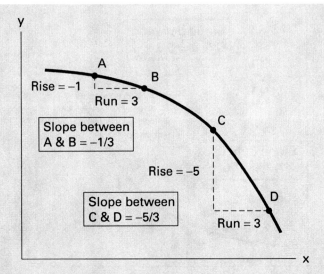

Figure 1.8c Negative and increasing slope.

The slope of this curve is negative—the values of *y* decrease as the values of *x* increase. The slope increases *in absolute value* as we move from left to right along the curve. Between points A and B, the slope is −1/3. Between points C and D, the slope is −5/3. Curves with negative and increasing slope are also sometimes called "concave to the origin."

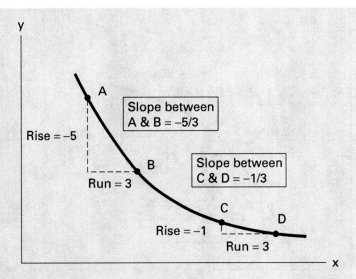

Figure 1.8d Negative and decreasing slope.

The slope of this curve is negative—the values of *y* decrease as the values of *x* increase. The slope decreases *in absolute value* as we move from left to right along the curve. Between points A and B, the slope is −5/3. Between points C and D, the slope is −1/3. Curves with negative and decreasing slope are also sometimes called "convex to the origin."

Figure 1.8d has a negative and decreasing (in absolute value) slope: y decreases as x increases, and the decreases in y get smaller and smaller as x increases. Figure 1.8d is also sometimes called **convex to the origin**. The slope between points C and D is smaller (in absolute value) than the slope between points A and B.

TRY

You need to be able to go back and forth between words and graphs. Try drawing a graph for each of the following statements:

5. Quantity demanded decreases as price increases (vertical axis: price; horizontal axis: quantity demanded).

6. Spending increases as wealth increases, but the increases in spending get smaller and smaller as wealth gets larger and larger (vertical axis: spending; horizontal axis: wealth).

7. As the number of workers increases, their marginal product first increases but then later decreases (vertical axis: marginal product; horizontal axis: number of workers).

8. Income always equals aggregate spending (vertical axis: aggregate spending; horizontal axis: income).

9. When the unemployment rate is low, the inflation rate is high but when the unemployment rate is high, the inflation rate is low (vertical axis: inflation rate; horizontal axis: unemployment rate).

10. Quantity supplied increases as price increases (vertical axis: price; horizontal axis: quantity supplied).

11. For a monopolist, as quantity increases, marginal revenue has a steeper negative slope than average revenue (vertical axis: marginal revenue and average revenue; horizontal axis: quantity). (You need to draw two curves.)

12. When the amount of butter produced is decreased from 2,000 to 1,900 units, the number of guns produced increases from 10 to 20 units. But when the amount of butter produced is decreased from 1,000 to 900 units, the number of guns produced increases from 80 to just 82 units (vertical axis: units of butter produced; horizontal axis: units of guns produced).

13. Quantity supplied is 13 when price is 5. But when price is 8, quantity supplied is 19 (vertical axis: price; horizontal axis: quantity supplied).

14. When price is 5, quantity demanded is 40. But when price is 10, quantity demanded is 30 (vertical axis: price; horizontal axis: quantity demanded).

TIP

Whenever you read about a relationship between two variables, sketch how it looks.

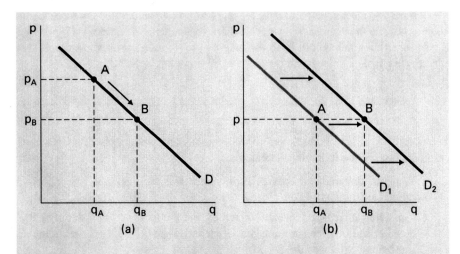

Figure 1.9 (a) Moving along a curve versus (b) shifting a curve.

When we go between two points on an existing curve, we are "moving along" the curve. In Figure 1.9a, as price *p* decreases, we move along the curve from A to B to a higher quantity *q*. When there is an entirely new curve, we are "shifting" the curve. In Figure 1.9b, at *every* price *p* there is an increase in quantity *q*, so there is an entirely new curve D_2.

Move Along versus Shift of a Curve

Economists are fond of the phrases **move along a curve** and **shift of a curve**. When we "move along" a curve, we are going between two points on an existing curve. In Figure 1.9a, if the price changes from p_A to p_B, quantity changes from q_A to q_B. We have moved along (or, in some books, slid along) the existing curve.

When the curve "shifts," the entire relationship between the two variables changes. In Figure 1.9b, if *at every price* there is an increase in quantity, the curve shifts from D_1 to D_2. In effect, the first curve D_1 ceases to exist. It sometimes helps to draw the new curve much darker than the initial curve.

An easy way to figure out whether we are moving along or shifting a curve is this: If an independent variable that is measured on one of the axes changes, we move along the existing curve. But if an independent variable that is *not* measured on one of the axes changes, the entire curve shifts.

CONCLUSION

This chapter has provided an overview of the mathematical tools used in economics. Refer back to this chapter as needed when tools are introduced and used. If you're still stuck, it might help to find a math book that provides more review. Now we are ready to get into some of the meat of economics.

Chapter 2

Production Possibilities Frontier, Economic Growth, and Gains from Trade

A simple but powerful model of the economy is the production possibilities frontier (PPF) model. Economic growth and the gains from trade can also be illustrated with the PPF.

KEY TERMS AND CONCEPTS

- Production possibilities frontier
- Resources
- Scarce resources
- Tradeoffs
- Opportunity cost
- Forego
- Law of increasing opportunity cost
- Attainable
- Efficient
- Inefficient
- Unattainable
- Economic growth
- Productivity
- Gains from trade
- Ricardian model
- Theory of comparative advantage
- Absolute advantage
- Comparative advantage

KEY GRAPHS

- PPF
- Shifts of PPF
- Straight-line PPF

KEY EQUATION

• Calculation of opportunity cost

THE PRODUCTION POSSIBILITIES FRONTIER

The **production possibilities frontier** (PPF) is a model about the allocation of scarce resources. It can be applied to a person or a company but is most often applied to an entire economy. What are the possible production combinations that an economy can produce with the available resources in a given time frame?

Resources are those things used to produce goods and services. Resources are broadly defined:

• labor or time
• capital (machines and buildings)
• land or natural resources
• knowledge or technology

Resources are said to be **scarce** because at any moment in time, there is a fixed, finite quantity of each resource. There are only 24 hours in a day, only a certain number of available workers, a certain number of machines and buildings, a certain amount of natural resources, a certain level of knowledge.

Resources must be allocated because if a resource—you, for instance—is used for one activity, it cannot simultaneously be used for another. In the next minute, you can study economics or you can study chemistry. You can't do both. The land under the building under your feet can be used for farming or for buildings, but not for both. So our resources must be allocated.

The PPF makes a key simplifying assumption: There are only two types of output. We can say some useful things about scarcity and resource allocation, even when we make such an unrealistic assumption. And we don't lose much of our story by making this assumption. So we make the assumption: only two types of output.

TIP

The PPF model always considers two types of output—never more, never fewer.

Because resources can't do everything simultaneously, we face tradeoffs, or choices. Land can be used to produce food or produce machines. If more land is devoted to growing food, then less land must be devoted to producing machines. Why? Because there is a limited amount of land.

If you are going to use the next hour to study economics, you can't use the next hour to study chemistry. You face a choice, or what economists call a **tradeoff**.

Economists call these tradeoffs **opportunity costs**. The opportunity cost of an activity is the next best alternative you **forego** (don't do) in order to do the activity. If you weren't studying economics, what would you rather be doing? That's your opportunity cost of studying economics.

Because resources—labor or time, capital, land or natural resources, knowledge or technology—are limited, every activity has an opportunity cost. Every one. In the PPF model, where there are only two possible activities, the opportunity cost of one activity is measured by the amount of the other activity foregone (not done).

The PPF is best illustrated with an example. The two outputs are guns (military items) and butter (nonmilitary items). If we use resources to produce guns, we are foregoing (not getting) production of butter. If our economy starts out producing, say, 10,000 guns per week and 50,000 pounds of butter per week, and we shift resources so that next week more guns are produced, then the opportunity cost of those additional guns will be the butter we can no longer produce.

One way to illustrate the point is with numbers. With the available resources, the economy can produce any of Table 2.1's combinations of guns and butter.

Table 2.1   Production Possibilities: Guns and Butter

Guns	0	5,000	10,000	15,000	20,000
Butter (lb)	75,000	65,000	50,000	30,000	0

How much butter do we forego (not produce) when gun production is increased from 10,000 to 15,000? Look at the numbers in the highlighted section of the table. We forego $50,000 - 30,000 = 20,000$ pounds of butter. So economists say: The opportunity cost of increasing gun production from 10,000 to 15,000 guns is 20,000 pounds of butter.

TRY

Try your hand at these problems.
Answers for all "TRY" problems are at the back of the book.

1. Using the numbers in Table 2.1, what is the opportunity cost of increasing gun production from 15,000 to 20,000?

2. Using the numbers in Table 2.1, what is the opportunity cost of increasing butter production from 65,000 pounds to 75,000 pounds?

Resources are not equally well suited to producing everything. An acre of land that produces desert cactus is not well suited to producing rice. A skilled electrician is not as well suited to designing clothing. A car is not well suited to plowing fields. Resources do some things better than others. Economists sometimes say: Resources are not ubiquitous.

Because resources are better suited to some activities than others, the opportunity cost of switching resources is not constant. If the economy starts out producing 10,000 guns and 50,000 pounds of butter, which resources should be shifted to gun production if more guns are wanted? The smart (economists say, efficient) thing to do is shift the resources away from butter production that are relatively worst at producing butter. That way the best (economists say, most efficient) resources are left to produce butter.

But if each time we want to increase gun production, we shift the resources away from butter that are relatively worst at producing butter, as we go along we start to move better and better butter producers over to gun production. And so we would have to give up more and more butter each time we shift resources from producing butter to producing guns. Economists call this the **law of increasing opportunity cost**.

The numbers in Table 2.1 illustrate this law. (When economists call something a "law," it means it is darn near always true.)

Shift resources so we are producing 5,000 rather than 0 guns, and the opportunity cost of those 5,000 guns is $75,000 - 65,000 = 10,000$ pounds of butter. But shift resources again so that now we are producing 10,000 rather than 5,000 guns, and now the opportunity cost of that second batch of 5,000 guns is $65,000 - 50,000 = 15,000$ pounds of butter.

Table 2.2 shows the opportunity cost of shifting resources toward gun production

Table 2.2   Opportunity Cost of Shifting From Butter to Gun Production

Guns	0		5,000		10,000		15,000		20,000
Butter foregone		10,000		15,000		20,000		30,000	

The opportunity cost of producing 5,000 guns rose from 10,000 to 15,000 to 20,000 to 30,000 pounds of butter. Because these numbers rise, the example illustrates the law of increasing opportunity cost.

When we draw a production possibilities frontier, all of these concepts are illustrated in one simple curved line.

Figure 2.1 shows the five points of Table 2.1 and connects the points with a smooth curve. That smooth curve is what we call the **production possibilities frontier**.

The PPF is drawn on a simple set of axes because there are just two types of output. The axes are the amount of each product produced in some time period. In our example, we have the number of guns and the amount of butter produced per week. The particular time period doesn't matter. What does matter is that you know the PPF is drawn for some particular finite time period.

The PPF shows tradeoffs by sloping down (it has a **negative slope**). The PPF shows the law of increasing opportunity costs by being curved (it is **nonlinear**). Economists often say the PPF is "bowed out" or "concave to the origin."

TIP

It doesn't matter which good is on which axis. Swap guns and butter. The PPF will still have the same shape—bowed out from the origin.

Table 2.3   Plotting a Production Possibilities Frontier

Guns	0	5,000	10,000	15,000	20,000
Butter (lb)	75,000	65,000	50,000	30,000	0
Label	A	B	C	D	E

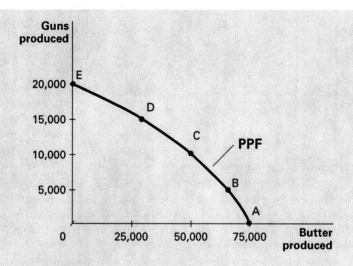

Figure 2.1 Production possibilities frontier for guns and butter.

The production possibilities frontier shows the combinations of output that can be produced with the available resources. Point A represents a combination of 75,000 pounds of butter and 0 guns. Point C represents a combination of 50,000 pounds of butter and 10,000 guns. Point E represents a combination of 0 pounds of butter and 20,000 guns.

TRY

For the next two problems, use these numbers

Rice (bu.)	0	5,000	8,000	10,000	11,000
Corn (bu.)	20,000	15,000	10,000	5,000	0

3. Draw the production possibilities frontier, putting corn on the vertical axis and rice on the horizontal axis.

4. Do these numbers illustrate the law of increasing opportunity cost?

Figure 2.2 shows what a PPF looks like in general, when we don't have any numbers to start from. It is downward sloping (higher on the left, lower on the right) because every activity has an opportunity cost. Producing more of one good

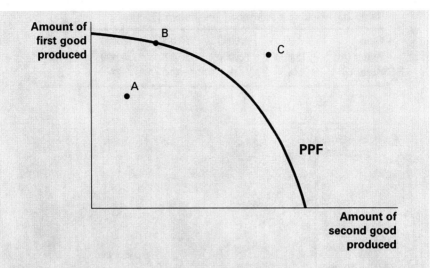

Figure 2.2 Production possibilities frontier.

The production possibilities frontier (PPF) is downward sloping because every activity has an opportunity cost. There are tradeoffs. If more of the second good is produced, less of the first good must be produced. The PPF is nonlinear. It is bowed out, which is also called concave to the origin. The opportunity cost of producing more of the second good is foregone production of the first good. As more of the second good is produced, the opportunity cost rises.

requires producing less of the other good. It is nonlinear (not a straight line), bowed out, or concave to the origin because of the law of increasing opportunity costs. Resources are not equally well suited to all tasks.

Any point between the axes and the PPF (such as point A in Figure 2.2) or on the PPF (such as point B) represents a combination of output that can be produced with the available resources; economists say these combinations are **attainable**. Any point *on* the PPF (such as B) is a combination of output that uses all the available resources; economists call those combinations **efficient**. Any point *inside but not on* the PPF (between the axes and the PPF, such as A) represents a combination of output that is not using all the available resources; those combinations are called **inefficient**. Any combination of output *outside of* the PPF (above or to the right, such as C) represents a combination of output that cannot be produced with the available resources; economists call those points **unattainable**.

TRY

5. Draw a PPF. Label four points on your graph:
   a. A combination of output that is attainable
   b. A combination of output that is efficient

    c. A combination of output that is inefficient

    d. A combination of output that is unattainable

6. Can a combination of output be simultaneously efficient and unattainable?

ECONOMIC GROWTH

The combinations of output outside of the current PPF can be attained if there is **economic growth**. Economic growth is defined here as an increase in the total amount of output that an economy can produce. (Growth will be defined at other times as an increase in the total amount of output per person: output divided by population.) Economic growth can occur two ways: more resources or more productive resources.

More resources—more people, more capital, more land, more natural resources—allows more output to be produced. The PPF shifts out. Usually the new PPF is pretty much parallel to the old one, as shown in Figure 2.3.

A decrease in available resources such as might happen in a natural disaster, drought, or famine has the opposite effect. The PPF shifts in, toward the axis, because if there are fewer available resources, then less output can be produced.

If resources are able to produce more output, economists say there has been an increase in **productivity**. Workers can produce more output in an hour if they have better training. Machinery can produce more output in an hour if it is engineered to

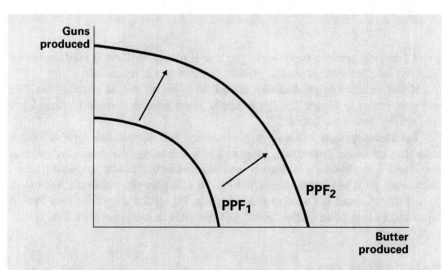

Figure 2.3 Economic growth.

Economic growth is shown by shifting out the production possibilities frontier. More resources means more of both guns and butter can be produced. The new production possibilities frontier, *PPF₂*, is above and to the right of the original production possibilities frontier, *PPF₁*.

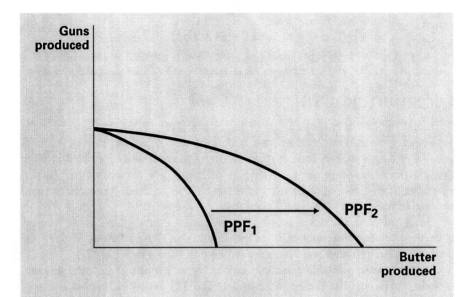

Figure 2.4 Asymmetric economic growth.
Sometimes economic growth affects some output but not others. A productivity increase that affects only butter (but not guns) means more butter can be produced but the maximum amount of guns does not change. The end point of the PPF on the butter axis shifts to the right, but the end point on the guns axis does not change. Connect the two new end points to get the new production possibilities frontier, *PPF₂*.

do so. Land can produce more output per acre if proper fertilizer is used. Increased productivity allows for economic growth: more output is produced.

If the increase in productivity affects all types of output equally, the PPF will shift out as in Figure 2.3. For example, more education could increase labor productivity across the board.

But sometimes an increase in productivity will impact one type of output more than another. For instance, suppose a new technology for producing butter is developed. It increases the maximum amount of butter that can be produced if all resources are used to produce butter but has no effect on the maximum amount of guns if all resources are used to produce guns. Figure 2.4 shows the new PPF. It starts at the same point on the "guns" axis but ends at a new point on the "butter" axis.

GAINS FROM TRADE

Another way to attain the unattainable—to have combinations of output that are beyond an economy's production possibilities frontier—is through trade. The idea of the **gains from trade** is that, collectively, more output can be produced if we specialize in producing the good we are relatively good at producing and then trade for other goods.

TIP

Some textbooks postpone this topic until the chapter on international trade. Others include it in the chapter on the production possibilities frontier.

When we all specialize, more output will be produced collectively than if we all try to be self-sufficient. Economists call this result the gains from trade. The idea is attributed to David Ricardo, a nineteenth-century British economist. Some economists call what we are about to do the "**Ricardian model**." Others refer to it as the **theory of comparative advantage**.

Gains from trade exist even if one economy is better than the other economy at producing everything. When one economy (or person) can produce some output with fewer resources than another, economists say the first economy has an **absolute advantage**.

It takes 20 hours of labor for Miranda to sew a dress but it takes only 8 hours of labor for Michael to sew the same dress. Economists say: Michael has the absolute advantage in the sewing of dresses. In this example, absolute advantage is determined by looking at the input required (hours of labor) to produce a certain output (a sewn dress).

Instead, we could just as easily look at the amount of output (number of sewn dresses) produced with a certain amount of inputs (a week of labor). In 40 hours, Miranda could sew two dresses and Michael could sew five dresses. This is the same example. Again, because Michael can produce more output with the same inputs, economists say: Michael has the absolute advantage in the sewing of dresses.

We do not care about absolute advantage when showing the gains from trade. To demonstrate that specialization and trade produces more output than self-sufficiency, we instead look at a concept economists call "comparative advantage." Comparative advantage depends on opportunity cost. Let's start there.

To show the gains from trade, we need some simplifications and an assumption. Simplifications:

- There are only two countries (or two people, or two states . . . the key is *two*).
- There are only two types of output.

Because of these simplifications, some economists say: We are looking at a 2 × 2 matrix of countries and outputs. What they mean is that if we were to construct a table—a matrix—with the countries down the side and the outputs along the top, we would have a table that is two cells wide and two cells high. For example, if Kern County and Taft County are the economies and corn and wheat are the outputs, we could put all of the information we need in a table such as Table 2.4.

Assumption:

- Opportunity costs are constant.

We ignore the law of increasing opportunity costs when showing the gains from trade. We can ignore this law because the results we will get—that there are

Table 2.4   An Output Table

Kern County's production of corn	Kern County's production of wheat
Taft County's production of corn	Taft County's production of wheat

gains from trade—are the same whether we do or don't have increasing opportunity costs. Our task is simpler if we let opportunity costs stay constant. Any assumption that makes our task simpler and doesn't change our conclusion is an assumption worth making!

The existence of gains from trade can really only be seen with an example. Our two economies are Kern County and Taft County. Our two outputs are corn and wheat. In a year, an acre of land in Kern County can produce 200 bushels of corn or 150 bushels of wheat. An acre of land in Taft County can produce 100 bushels of corn or 50 bushels of wheat per year. Economists usually present this information in a table such as Table 2.5.

Table 2.5   Maximum Annual Production per Acre

	Corn	Wheat
Kern County	200 bu.	150 bu.
Taft County	100 bu.	50 bu.

TRY

Use Table 2.5 to answer these questions.

7. Which economy has the absolute advantage in the production of corn?

8. Which economy has the absolute advantage in the production of wheat?

With this information, we can calculate the opportunity costs for each economy. An acre of land can be used *either* for corn *or* for wheat, but not for both. The opportunity cost of corn is the amount of wheat foregone (not produced). The opportunity cost of wheat is the amount of corn foregone (not produced). We use the information on production possibilities to calculate the opportunity costs.

$$\textit{Opportunity cost of good A} = \frac{\textit{maximum production of other good}}{\textit{maximum production of good A}}$$

In Kern County, the opportunity cost of 200 bushels of corn is 150 bushels of wheat. Divide by 200 to get the opportunity cost of 1 bushel of corn. The opportunity cost of 1 bushel of corn in Kern County is $150/200 = 3/4$, or 0.75 bushels of wheat.

In Kern County, the opportunity cost of 150 bushels of wheat is 200 bushels of corn. Divide by 150: the opportunity cost of 1 bushel of wheat in Kern County is 200/150 = 4/3, or 1.33 bushels of wheat.

TIP

Notice that the opportunity cost of one good (wheat) is just the reciprocal of the opportunity cost of the other good (corn).

In Taft County, the opportunity cost of 100 bushels of corn is 50 bushels of wheat. Divide by 100: the opportunity cost of 1 bushel of corn in Taft County is 100/50 = 2 bushels of wheat.

Flip it over: The opportunity cost of 1 bushel of wheat in Taft County is 1/2 bushel of corn.

Economists usually present this information in a table such as Table 2.6.

Table 2.6   Opportunity Costs of 1 Bushel of . . .

	. . . Corn	. . . Wheat
Kern County	150/200 = 0.75 bu. of wheat per bu. of corn	200/150 = 1.33 bu. of corn per bu. of wheat
Taft County	50/100 = 0.5 bu. of wheat per bu. of corn	100/50 = 2 bu. of corn per bu. of wheat

---

TIP

To be sure you get the right ratio, it helps to include the entire phrase such as "bushels of wheat per bushel of corn." In this case, the numerator has "bushels of wheat"; the denominator has "bushels of corn."

Opportunity costs are used to determine comparative advantage. The economy with the lower opportunity cost has what economists call the **comparative advantage** in the production of that good.

To produce a bushel of corn, Kern County gives up 0.75 bushels of wheat but Taft County gives up only 0.5 bushels of wheat. So economists say: Taft County has the comparative advantage in the production of corn.

To produce a bushel of wheat, Kern County gives up 1.33 bushels of corn and Taft County gives up fully 2 bushels of corn. Economists would say: Kern County has the comparative advantage in the production of wheat.

To determine the total possible production of corn and of wheat, we need to know how many acres are available in each economy. Let's assume there are 300

Table 2.7   Maximum Annual Production per Economy

	Corn	Wheat
Kern County	200 bu. per acre × 300 acres = 60,000 bu.	150 bu. per acre × 300 acres = 45,000 bu.
Taft County	100 bu. per acre × 300 acres = 30,000 bu.	50 bu. per acre × 300 acres = 15,000 bu.

available acres in Kern County and 300 available acres in Taft County. The total maximum possible production is shown in Table 2.7.

TIP

Confusion alert! The table is saying that Kern County can produce a maximum of 60,000 bushels of corn *or* 45,000 bushels of wheat. "Or" not "and."

The production possibilities can be shown in a graph. Each economy gets its own graph. In Kern County, 60,000 bushels of corn *or* 45,000 bushels of wheat *or* any combination of corn and wheat in between can be produced. In Taft County, 30,000 bushels of corn *or* 15,000 bushels of wheat *or* any combination of corn and wheat in between can be produced. Figure 2.5 shows these production possibilities.

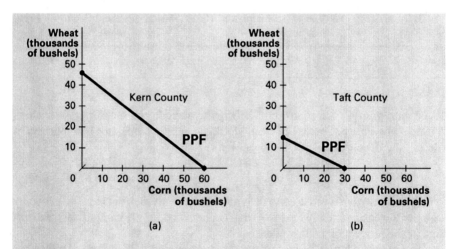

(a)   (b)

Figure 2.5 Production possibilities frontiers for Kern and Taft Counties.
In Kern County, the production possibilities are 45,000 bushes of wheat and no bushels of corn, 60,000 bushels of corn and no bushels of wheat, or any combination in between. In Taft County, the production possibilities are 15,000 bushes of wheat and no bushels of corn, 30,000 bushels of corn and no bushels of wheat, or any combination in between. Because we assume constant opportunity costs, the production possibilities frontiers are straight lines.

The PPFs are straight lines because we assume the opportunity costs shown in Table 2.6 do not change.

The graphs can be used to calculate opportunity costs. Say the same thing another way: the slope of the production possibilities frontiers is the opportunity cost. The slope of the PPF is rise/run, or Δwheat/Δcorn. In Kern County, the slope of the PPF is $45/60 = 0.75$. This is the opportunity cost of a bushel of corn in Kern County.

The slope of the PPF in Taft County is $15/30 = 0.5$. This is the opportunity cost of a bushel of corn in Taft County.

TIP

You simply have to memorize that the slope is the opportunity cost of the good on the horizontal axis (the denominator of the slope equation), measured in units foregone of the good on the vertical axis (the numerator of the slope equation).

Now we need to choose some current level of production for both Kern and Taft Counties. Typically economists choose a point somewhere near the middle of the PPF of each economy. Let's assume Kern County is producing 18,000 bushels of corn and 31,500 bushels of wheat, a point on its PPF. And let's assume Taft County is producing 6,000 bushels of corn and 12,000 bushels of wheat.

TIP

Showing the gains from trade requires that you (or your book, or your instructor) make assumptions like these about each economy's production possibilities and current levels of production.

Total worldwide production is just the sum of production in each economy.

Each economy should specialize in producing the good in which it has the comparative advantage. Kern County has the lower opportunity cost—the comparative advantage—in producing wheat, so it should use all of its resources to produce wheat. Kern County will produce 45,000 bushels of wheat (see Table 2.7).

Taft County has the lower opportunity cost—the comparative advantage—in producing corn. So Taft County should use all of its resources to produce corn. Taft County will produce 30,000 bushels of corn.

Table 2.8   Total Production Without Specialization

	Corn	Wheat
Kern County	18,000	31,500
Taft County	6,000	12,000
Total Production	24,000	43,500

Total production of wheat has increased! Without specialization, Kern and Taft Counties were together producing 43,500 bushels of wheat. With specialization, they are producing 45,000 bushels of wheat. There is a gain of 1,500 bushels of wheat.

Total production of corn has also increased! Without specialization, Kern and Taft Counties were together producing 24,000 bushels of corn. With specialization, they are producing 30,000 bushels of corn. There is a gain of 6,000 bushels of corn.

Kern and Taft Counties can now trade wheat for corn. The result is that both can consume more corn and wheat, with specialization and trade, than they could when each economy was self-sufficient. Economists say: This result demonstrates the gains from trade.

TRY

9. When economists say there are "gains from trade," what is being gained?

10. There are two people, Robin and Marian. Marian is relatively better than Robin at gardening. Robin is relatively better than Marian at cooking. But Robin is better than Marian at doing everything. Will Robin and Marian gain from trading? Who should do what?

Chapter 3

Demand and Supply

The model of demand and supply is used to determine the price of a product. It is the most often used model in economics. Success in economics depends on mastering the model of demand and supply.

KEY TERMS AND CONCEPTS

- Model of demand and supply
- Good
- Service
- Market
- Demand
- Supply
- Equilibrium price
- Equilibrium quantity
- Quantity demanded
- Market demand
- Individual demand
- Demand schedule
- Demand curve
- Move along a curve
- Shift of a curve
- Complementary goods
- Substitute goods
- Income
- Normal good
- Inferior goods
- Wealth
- Tastes and preferences
- Quantity supplied
- Market supply
- Individual supply
- Supply schedule
- Supply curve

- Substitutes in production
- Complements in production
- Market equilibrium
- Market shortage
- Market surplus

KEY GRAPHS

- Equilibrium in a market
- Shift of demand
- Shift of supply

OVERVIEW OF MODEL OF DEMAND AND SUPPLY

The **model of demand and supply** is used over and over in economics. This model answers the question: What determines the price and quantity sold in the market for a product? The product may be a **good**, a tangible product such as a pen, house, book, or shirt. Or the product may be a **service**, an intangible such as a doctor's appointment, a haircut, computer repair, or DVD rental. A **market** is not a physical place. It is instead the collection of the actions of the buyers and sellers of a product.

Demand captures the behavior of buyers. There are many factors that may influence the quantity or amount of a product that we wish to purchase. Economists usually identify five factors that influence buyer demand:

- the item's price
- the prices of other items we could use with or instead of this product
- our income
- our wealth
- our tastes or preferences

Supply captures the behavior of sellers. As with demand, there are many factors that may influence the quantity of a product that sellers wish to sell. Economists usually identify four factors that influence seller supply:

- the item's price
- costs of inputs
- productivity of inputs
- the prices of other items that could be produced with the same inputs

The item's price matters to both buyers and sellers. The interaction of demand and supply determine the **equilibrium price** and **equilibrium quantity** of the product. At the equilibrium price, the quantity of the product buyers wish to purchase (called quantity demanded) equals the quantity of the product sellers wish to sell (called quantity supplied). Economists often say: Prices depend on supply and demand.

DEMAND

We focus first on price. **Quantity demanded** is the quantity associated with any one particular price. The many combinations of possible price and related quantity demanded make up the demand for the product. Demand refers to all the combinations of price and quantity demanded. **Market demand** for a product is the sum of everyone's **individual demand**.

How does a change in price affect the quantity of a product that buyers wish to buy? When prices rise, buyers don't want to buy as much. Economists say: An increase in price lowers quantity demanded. When the price of a product falls, buyers want to buy more. Economists say: A decrease in price raises quantity demanded.

TIP

"Demand" and "quantity demanded" are different. It is very important that you do not mix up the two.

The relationship between price and quantity demanded can be depicted in a table that economists often call a **demand schedule**. Let's suppose we survey all potential buyers of spiral notebooks. We ask each person: How many 100-page one-subject spiral notebooks will you purchase in a semester if spiral notebooks cost 50 cents each? What if they cost $1.00 each? $1.50 each? $2.00 each? $2.50 each? We add up the individual demand (each person's response) at each price. This gives us the market demand, which is in Table 3.1.

Table 3.1   Demand Schedule

Price	50¢	$1.00	$1.50	$2.00	$2.50
Quantity demanded	10,000	8,000	6,000	4,000	2,000
Label	A	B	C	D	E

Demand can also be depicted in a graph. Price is always shown on the vertical axis. Quantity is always shown on the horizontal axis. You may be bothered by this. You may want to argue that since we said price determines quantity demanded, price should be shown on the horizontal axis. Don't. Everyone, everywhere, plots price on the vertical axis and quantity on the horizontal axis.

TIP

For the supply and demand model, price is *always* shown on the vertical axis. Quantity is *always* shown on the horizontal axis. Memorize this.

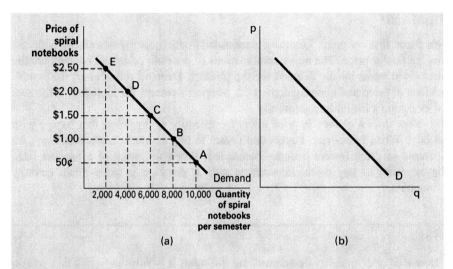

Figure 3.1 Demand curves slope down.

The demand curve for spiral notebooks in Figure 3.1a is based on the combinations of price and quantity demanded in Table 3.1. In general, a demand curve is a downward-sloping curve, as shown in Figure 3.1b.

Figure 3.1a shows the **demand curve** for spiral notebooks. Each combination of price and quantity demanded in Table 3.1 is plotted and labeled. A smooth curve connects the five points. This is our demand curve. The demand curve slopes down. It has this negative slope because there is an inverse relationship between price and quantity demanded. In general, demand curves are downward sloping—when you draw a demand curve, you start from the upper left and go down to the lower right—as shown in Figure 3.1b.

TIP

Economists say: Demand curves slope down (have a negative slope) because there is an inverse relationship between price and quantity demanded. This means demand curves slope down because when the price is lower, quantity demanded is higher.

If the price of the product changes, we **move along** the demand curve. Different price? Go to a different point on the same demand curve. But if any of the other four factors that affect demand changes, then the entire demand curve will **shift**. That is, at each possible price of the product, there will be a change in the quantity demanded. There will be a whole new curve. Figure 3.2 illustrates.

Prices of Other Products

Items that we use *with* the product are called **complementary goods**. Pens are complements to spiral notebooks. In general, when the price of a complementary

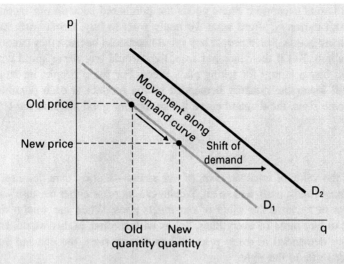

Figure 3.2 Movement along versus shift of a demand curve.

A movement along the demand curve occurs when the good's price changes. When the price changes from the "old price" to the "new price," we move along the demand curve, D_1, from the "old quantity" to the "new quantity." But if something *other than the good's price* changes, the entire demand curve shifts. At every price, there is a new quantity demanded, which is shown as a second demand curve, D_2.

good rises, we buy less of both the complement and the initial product. If pens triple in price, some people will start taking class notes on a laptop rather than in a spiral notebook, lowering the quantity demanded of spiral notebooks at each possible price. The entire demand curve for spiral notebooks shifts to the left. Economists say: When the price of a complement (the pen) rises, demand for the primary product (the spiral notebook) falls.

Items we use *instead* of the product are called **substitute goods**. Loose-leaf filler paper and binders are substitutes for spiral notebooks. In general, when the price of a substitute good rises, we buy more of the initial product. If binders triple in price, some people will stop using loose-leaf filler paper and binders and will instead start taking class notes in a spiral notebook, raising the quantity demanded of spiral notebooks at each possible price. The entire demand curve for spiral notebooks shifts to the right. Economists say: When the price of a substitute (binder and paper) rises, demand for the primary product (the spiral notebook) rises.

Income

Income is what we receive for working. When our income rises, we can afford to buy more of everything. In general, increased income raises the quantity demanded of a product at each possible price. If we want to buy more of a good when our income rises, economists call the good a **normal good**. Regardless of the price, we will buy more music after our income rises than we did before. When income rises, the demand curve for a normal good shifts to the right.

There is one exception: Some goods are purchased because our income is so low we can't currently afford what we really want to buy. Economists call these goods **inferior goods**. Some people buy spiral notebooks because they cannot afford to buy a laptop. But if their incomes rose, they would buy fewer spiral notebooks and instead buy a laptop for taking class notes. For these people, an increase in income will lower the quantity demanded of the product at each possible price. When income rises, the demand curve for an inferior good shifts to the left.

Wealth

Wealth is the value of what we own, of our assets—houses, cars, jewelry, stocks, bonds, mutual funds, cash, and so on. Wealth can increase either because we obtain more assets or because the value of our assets rises. When our wealth rises, we can afford to buy more of everything. So, as with income, higher wealth increases the quantity demanded at every price. When wealth rises, the demand curve for the product shifts to the right.

Tastes or Preferences

Apart from prices, income, and wealth, sometimes we just *like* a product and want to buy it. Sometimes we learn of a product through advertising and decide to buy it. Or a friend plays some music and we decide to download it, too. Economists call this the influence of tastes or preferences. **Tastes and preferences** is a catch-all phrase that captures the multitude of reasons other than prices, income, and wealth that we may decide we want more or less of a product. If our tastes shift in favor of an item, at every possible price there is a higher quantity demanded. The demand curve shifts to the right. If our tastes shift away from the item, demand shifts to the left.

Size of Market

One additional factor that shifts the market demand curve is the size of the market. If college enrollment increases, more individuals will want to purchase spiral notebooks. The market demand curve will shift to the right.

SUPPLY

Sellers' behavior is captured with the supply curve. **Quantity supplied** is the quantity associated with any one particular price. The many combinations of price and quantity supplied make up the supply of the product. **Market supply** of a product is the sum of every seller's **individual supply**.

When the price of an item rises, sellers want to sell more of that item. Economists say: An increase in price raises quantity supplied. When the price of the item falls, sellers want to sell less. Economists say: A decrease in price lowers quantity supplied.

TIP

"Supply" and "quantity supplied" are different. Do not mix them up.

Table 3.2 Supply Schedule

Price	50¢	$1.00	$1.50	$2.00	$2.50
Quantity supplied	4,000	5,000	6,000	7,000	8,000
Label	V	W	X	Y	Z

As with demand, the relationship between price and quantity supplied can be depicted in a table that economists call a **supply schedule**. Let's suppose we survey all the potential sellers of spiral notebooks. We ask each seller: How many 100-page one-subject spiral notebooks will you want to sell in a semester if you can sell spiral notebooks for 50 cents each? What if you can sell them for $1.00 each? $1.50 each? $2.00 each? $2.50 each? We add up the individual supply (each firm's responses) at each price. This gives us the market supply, which is in Table 3.2.

Supply can also be depicted in a graph. Price is again on the vertical axis. Quantity is on the horizontal axis. Figure 3.3 shows the **supply curve** for spiral notebooks. Each combination of price and quantity supplied in Table 3.2 is plotted and labeled in Figure 3.3a. A smooth curve—the supply curve—connects the five points.

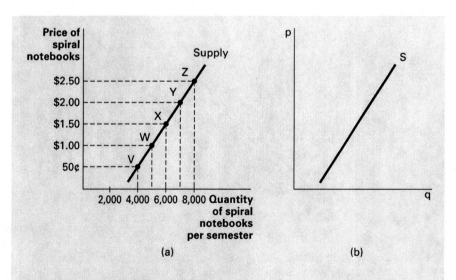

(a)

(b)

Figure 3.3 Supply curves slope up.

The supply curve for spiral notebooks in Figure 3.3a is based on the combinations of price and quantity supplied in Table 3.2. In general, a supply curve is upward sloping, as shown in Figure 3.3b.

A general supply curve is shown in Figure 3.3b. The supply curve slopes up. When you draw the supply curve, you start from the bottom left and go to the upper right. The supply curve has a positive slope because there is a direct relationship between price and quantity supplied. When price is higher, quantity supplied is higher. When price is lower, quantity supplied is lower.

TIP

Here's a trick to help remember which curve is which. **D**emand slopes **D**own. **Su**pply slopes **up**.

If the price of the product changes, we move along the existing supply curve to a different quantity supplied. But if either of the other factors that affect supply changes, the entire supply curve shifts. At each possible price, due to a change in one of these factors, there will be a change in quantity supplied. There is a whole new supply curve. See Figure 3.4.

Costs of Inputs

When it costs more to produce an item, sellers will not want to sell as much output at each possible price. If higher wages are paid to employees in the spiral notebook

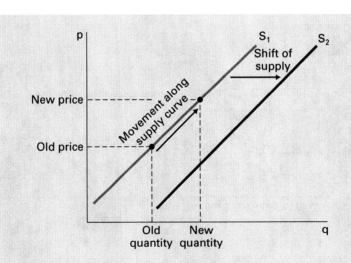

Figure 3.4 Movement along versus shift of a supply curve.

A movement along the supply curve occurs when the good's price changes. When the price changes from the "old price" to the "new price," we move along the supply curve, S_1, from the "old quantity" to the "new quantity." But if something *other than the good's price* changes, the entire supply curve shifts. At every price, there is a new quantity supplied, which is shown as a second supply curve, S_2.

factory, sellers of spiral notebooks will not want to produce and sell as many note-books, lowering the quantity supplied at every possible price of spiral notebooks. The entire supply curve of spiral notebooks will shift to the left. Economists will say: Supply decreased.

Another way to get the same result is this. When it costs more to produce an item, sellers will want to charge a higher price. Any particular quantity supplied will be associated with a higher price as a result of the increased cost of inputs. The supply curve shifts up, which looks the same as the supply curve shifting left.

One reason we don't typically explain the impact of higher input costs this way is that it is too easy to get confused. The new supply curve is *above* the old supply curve. The supply curve seems to have moved *up*. But at every price, there is a lower quantity supplied. Economists say: When the cost of inputs rises, supply of the product goes *down*.

TIP

Here's one way to be sure your shift of the supply curve is drawn correctly. Draw the first (old) supply curve. Then draw an arrow *that is parallel to the horizontal axis* to show which way to shift the supply curve. If you are increasing supply, your arrow will point to the right. If you are decreasing supply, your arrow will point to the left. Finally, draw the second (new) supply curve at the end of your arrow. If your arrows go left or right (never up or down, never on the diagonal), you'll never be in the wrong!

Productivity of Inputs

When inputs are more productive, producing more for each input, the costs of producing the output fall. If the machines that bind the notebooks can run at a faster pace so more notebooks are produced per hour, sellers of spiral notebooks will be willing to supply a greater quantity at every possible price of spiral notebooks. The entire supply curve of spiral notebooks shifts to the right. Economists say: Increased productivity increases supply.

Prices of Related Output

Items that can be produced *instead* of the current output but using the same inputs are called **substitutes in production**. Lined paper is a substitute in production for spiral notebooks—it can be produced *instead* of spiral notebooks with many of the same inputs. In general, when the price of a substitute in production rises, firms will want to produce more of that item and less of the initial output. They will shift their inputs to producing the now-higher-priced substitute in production, and will produce less of the initial product. If lined paper doubles in price, many firms will produce fewer spiral notebooks and more lined paper. At every possible price of spiral notebooks, the quantity of spiral notebooks supplied will decline. The entire supply curve of spiral notebooks will shift to the left. Economists say: When the price of a substitute in production (lined paper) rises, supply of the primary product (spiral notebooks) falls.

t can be produced *with* the current output and using the same inputs are **ments in production**, or byproducts. Paper confetti is a complement to spiral notebooks—the three holes punched out of each sheet become confetti! In general when the price of a complement in production rises, firms will want to produce more of both the complement and the initial output. If confetti triples in price, spiral notebook producers will want to produce more confetti *and* more spiral notebooks. At every possible price of spiral notebooks, the quantity supplied will rise. The entire supply curve will shift to the right. Economists say: When the price of a complement in production (confetti) rises, supply of the primary product (spiral notebooks) rises.

Size of Market

One additional factor that shifts the supply curve is the number of sellers in the market. If more office supply stores open in the community, more sellers will want to sell spiral notebooks at each price. The entire supply curve shifts to the right.

EQUILIBRIUM

Market equilibrium occurs when the market finds the price where quantity demanded equals quantity supplied. At that price, every buyer who is willing and able to purchase the item is able to do so. And at that price, every seller who is willing and able to sell the item is able to do so. There are no buyers and no sellers unable to do what they are willing to do. Economists say: The market is in equilibrium when quantity demanded equals quantity supplied.

We can use the demand and supply schedules to find equilibrium. Table 3.3 combines the information from Tables 3.1 and 3.2.

When spiral notebooks sell for $1.50, quantity demanded and quantity supplied both equal 6,000 spiral notebooks per semester. The **equilibrium price** in this market is $1.50 per spiral notebook. The **equilibrium quantity** is 6,000 spiral notebooks per semester.

When the price is below the equilibrium price, quantity demanded exceeds quantity supplied. Economists call this difference between quantity demanded and quantity supplied a **market shortage**. When spiral notebooks are priced at $1.00

Table 3.3 Demand and Supply Schedules

Price	50¢	$1.00	$1.50	$2.00	$2.50
Quantity demanded	10,000	8,000	6,000	4,000	2,000
Quantity supplied	4,000	5,000	6,000	7,000	8,000
Shortage or surplus or equilibrium?	Shortage of 6,000	Shortage of 3,000	Equilibrium	Surplus of 3,000	Surplus of 6,000

each, quantity demanded of 8,000 notebooks exceeds quantity supplied of 5,000 notebooks. The market shortage is 3,000 spiral notebooks per semester. A market shortage puts upward pressure on prices.

When the price is above the equilibrium price, quantity supplied exceeds quantity demanded. Economists call this difference a **market surplus**. When spiral notebooks are priced at $2.50 each, quantity supplied of 8,000 notebooks exceeds quantity demanded of 2,000 notebooks. The market surplus is 6,000 spiral notebooks per semester. A market surplus puts downward pressure on prices.

When the market is in equilibrium, there is no market shortage and no market surplus. Quantity demanded equals quantity supplied. There is no pressure for price to change.

Market equilibrium is most often shown with a graph. Figure 3.5a on page 42 shows the market for spiral notebooks. The equilibrium point is where the demand and supply curves cross (or, intersect). If the price is above the equilibrium price, the market surplus is the horizontal distance between the demand curve and the supply curve at that too-high price. If the price is below the equilibrium price, the market shortage is the horizontal distance between the demand curve and the supply curve at that too-low price. In general, Figure 3.5b shows how economists use supply and demand curves to find the equilibrium price and equilibrium quantity.

Changes of Equilibrium

The power of the model of demand and supply comes from its ability to predict how equilibrium price and equilibrium quantity will change when one of the many factors that affect demand or supply change. Here it is especially important to keep straight the difference between a movement along and a shift of a curve. If the price changes, we move along an existing curve. If some other factor changes, a curve will shift.

Shift of Demand

When there is a change in prices of related goods, income, wealth, tastes or preferences, or the size of the market, the demand curve shifts. There is a new quantity demanded associated with each possible price. The old equilibrium price and quantity will no longer clear the market. Equilibrium price and equilibrium quantity will change.

When demand increases as in Figure 3.6a on page 43, the entire demand curve shifts to the right. At the initial price p_1, there is now a market shortage. Prices rise. As prices rise, sellers *move along* their supply curve, increasing quantity supplied. The market will settle at a new equilibrium with a higher equilibrium price and higher equilibrium quantity. Economists say: An increase in demand causes both prices and quantities to increase.

When demand decreases as in Figure 3.6b, the entire demand curve shifts to the left. At the initial equilibrium price p_1, there is now a market surplus. Because the demand curve shifted, quantity demanded is now less than quantity supplied at the old equilibrium price. Prices fall. As prices fall, sellers *move along* their supply

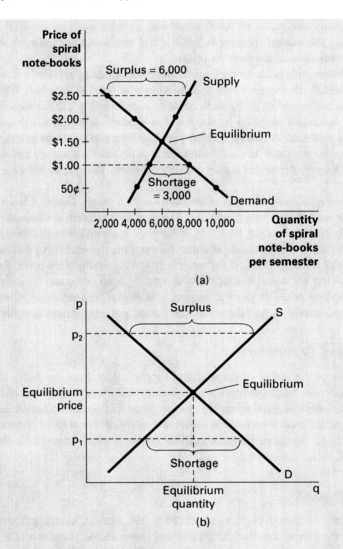

Figure 3.5 Market equilibrium.

Equilibrium in the market for spiral notebooks in Figure 3.5a occurs at a price of $1.50 and a quantity of 6,000. In general, market equilibrium occurs where the demand and supply curves intersect as shown in Figure 3.5b. When price is above the equilibrium price, there is a market surplus. When price is below the equilibrium price, there is a market shortage.

curve, and quantity supplied falls. The market will settle at a new equilibrium with a lower equilibrium price and lower equilibrium quantity. Economists say: A decrease in demand causes both prices and quantities to decrease.

Shift of Supply

When there is a change in costs of inputs, productivity, the prices of related output, or the number of sellers, the supply curve shifts. There is a new quantity supplied

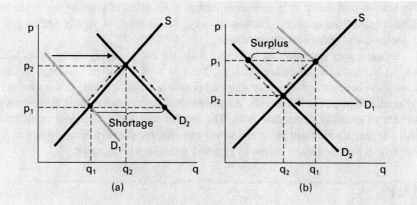

Figure 3.6 Shift of demand.

In Figure 3.6a, demand increases from D_1 to D_2. At the initial price p_1, there is a market shortage. Equilibrium price rises to p_2 and equilibrium quantity rises to q_2. In Figure 3.6b, demand decreases from D_1 to D_2. At the initial price p_1, there is a market surplus. Equilibrium price falls to p_2 and equilibrium quantity falls to q_2.

associated with each possible price. The old equilibrium price and quantity will no longer clear the market. Equilibrium price and equilibrium quantity will change.

When supply increases as in Figure 3.7a, the entire supply curve shifts to the right. At the initial price p_1, there is now a market surplus. Prices fall. As prices fall, buyers *move along* their demand curve, increasing quantity demanded.

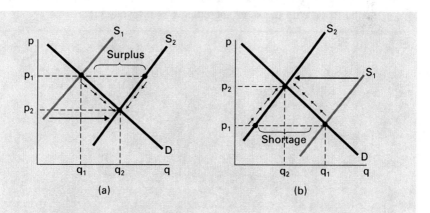

Figure 3.7 Shift of supply.

In Figure 3.7a, supply increases from S_1 to S_2. When supply increases, the supply curve shifts to the right. At the initial price p_1, there is a market surplus. Equilibrium price falls to p_2 and equilibrium quantity rises to q_2. In Figure 3.7b, supply decreases from S_1 to S_2. When supply decreases, the supply curve shifts to the left. At the initial price p_1, there is a market shortage. Equilibrium price rises to p_2 and equilibrium quantity falls to q_2.

The market will settle at a new equilibrium with a lower equilibrium price and higher equilibrium quantity. Economists say: An increase in supply causes prices to decrease and quantities to increase.

When supply decreases as in Figure 3.7b, the entire supply curve shifts to the left. At the initial equilibrium price p_1, there is now a market shortage. Because the supply curve shifted, quantity supplied is now less than quantity demanded at the old equilibrium price. Prices rise. As prices rise, buyers *move along* their demand curve, and quantity demanded falls. The market will settle at a new equilibrium with a higher equilibrium price and lower equilibrium quantity. Economists say: A decrease in supply causes prices to rise and quantities to decrease.

TRY

Answers to all "Try" questions are at the back of the book.

Use a graph of supply and demand to determine how each event affects equilibrium price and equilibrium quantity.

1. In the market for laptops, buyer income rises.
2. In the market for pens, wages of pen manufacturers rise.
3. In the market for hybrid cars, buyer preferences shift toward hybrids.
4. In the market for SUVs, the price of gasoline rises.
5. In the market for restaurant meals, more restaurants open in town.
6. In the market for crude oil, hurricanes destroy dozens of oil rigs.
7. In the market for a town's rental apartments, the town's population increases.
8. In the market for brownies, the price of chocolate truffle cookies (which can be made with the same ingredients as brownies) increases.

Chapter 4

Extensions of the Demand and Supply Model

Several extensions of the demand and supply model are common in principles of economics courses. In this chapter we look at how to model price floors and ceilings, and excise taxes. Elasticity—the responsiveness of something to changes in something else—and the concepts of consumer surplus, producer surplus, and deadweight loss are also covered.

KEY TERMS AND CONCEPTS

- Price floor
- Binding
- Price ceiling
- Inefficient
- Excise tax
- Burden of the tax
- Bears the burden
- Elasticity
- Price elasticity of demand
- Income elasticity of demand
- Cross-price elasticity of demand
- Perfectly inelastic demand
- Perfectly elastic demand
- Inelastic
- Elastic
- Unitary elasticity
- Midpoint method
- Total revenue effect
- Consumer surplus
- Producer surplus
- Total surplus
- Deadweight loss
- Deadweight loss of the tax

KEY EQUATIONS

- Elasticity
- Midpoint formula
- Consumer surplus
- Producer surplus
- Deadweight loss of a tax

KEY GRAPHS

- Price floor
- Price ceiling
- Excise tax
- Consumer surplus
- Producer surplus
- Deadweight loss of a tax

PRICE FLOORS AND PRICE CEILINGS

The model of demand and supply says that prices are determined "in the market" —by the interaction of buyers (demand) and sellers (supply). But what happens if there are government-imposed restrictions on the price?

A **price floor** exists when the market price is not allowed to fall below the floor, below a specific price. So a price floor is the lowest value a price can take. The market determines the price so long as the price remains above the floor. If market forces would push the price below the floor, then the price floor is **binding**.

When a price floor is binding, the market is not in equilibrium. The price is above the equilibrium price. As price rises above equilibrium, quantity demanded falls and quantity supplied rises. Quantity demanded is less than quantity supplied if the price equals the price floor. A graph helps.

Figure 4.1a shows a price floor. The equilibrium price, where the demand and supply curves cross, is below the price floor. So the price will be set at the price floor. At the price floor, quantity supplied exceeds quantity demanded. There is a market surplus.

If there was no price floor, the market surplus would put downward pressure on price. The price would fall until it reached the equilibrium price, where quantity demanded equals quantity supplied. But the existence of the price floor prevents the price from falling.

At the price floor, the quantity sold will be the quantity demanded. This quantity is below the equilibrium quantity.

Figure 4.1b shows a price floor that is not binding. The market equilibrium price is above the floor, so the market—supply and demand—determines the market price.

A **price ceiling** exists when the market price is not allowed to rise above the ceiling, above a specific price. So a price ceiling is the highest value a price can take. The market determines the price so long as the price remains below the

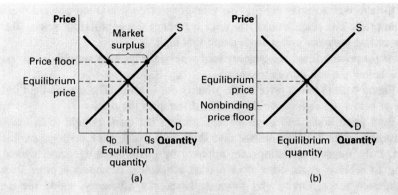

Figure 4.1 A price floor.

When a price floor is binding as in Figure 4.1a, quantity supplied exceeds quantity demanded, creating a market surplus. When the price floor is less than the equilibrium price as in Figure 4.1b, the price floor is nonbinding.

ceiling. If market forces would push the price above the ceiling, then the price ceiling is binding.

When a price ceiling is binding, the market is not in equilibrium. The price is below the equilibrium price. As price falls below equilibrium, quantity demanded rises and quantity supplied falls. So quantity demanded exceeds quantity supplied when the price is restricted to the price ceiling.

Figure 4.2a shows a price ceiling. The equilibrium price, where demand and supply cross, is above the price ceiling. The price will be set at the price ceiling. Quantity demanded, q_D, exceeds quantity supplied, q_S. There is a market shortage at the price ceiling.

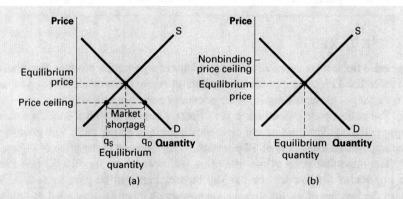

Figure 4.2 A price ceiling.

When a price ceiling is binding as in Figure 4.2a, quantity demanded exceeds quantity supplied, creating a market shortage. When a price ceiling is greater than the equilibrium price as in Figure 4.2b, it is nonbinding.

If there was no price ceiling, the market shortage would put upward pressure on the price. The price would rise until it reaches the equilibrium price. But the price ceiling prevents prices from rising that high.

At the price ceiling, the quantity sold will be the quantity supplied. This quantity is below the equilibrium quantity.

Figure 4.2b shows a price ceiling that is not binding. The market equilibrium price is below the ceiling. So the market determines the price.

Both price floors and price ceilings prevent the quantity sold from reaching equilibrium quantity. Economists say: Price floors and price ceilings are **inefficient**. Price floors and ceilings are imposed by government agencies, which are trying to achieve goals other than market efficiency. A common price floor is a minimum wage. Equity and fairness issues, not efficiency, guide the determination of the minimum wage. A common price ceiling is the price of milk, which is regulated in many states. California's website says it sets a price ceiling for milk because "[w]ithout economic regulation, a strong potential exists for volatile and chaotic production and marketing practices [of milk]." [Source: http://dairy.ca.gov/dairy_questions_main.html#4, accessed 3/27/07.]

TRY

Answers to all "Try" questions are at the back of the book.

Draw a graph that depicts each of the following. Is the price floor or ceiling binding? Will the market equilibrium quantity be sold?

1. The equilibrium price is $3 and the price floor is $4.
2. The equilibrium price is $3 and the price floor is $2.
3. The equilibrium price is $3 and the price ceiling is $5.
4. The equilibrium price is $3 and the price ceiling is $1.

EXCISE TAXES

An **excise tax** is a tax assessed on the purchase of a particular product. For example, the federal and most state governments impose excise taxes on alcohol and tobacco. A tax changes an item's equilibrium price and equilibrium quantity.

The easiest way to see how a tax affects a market is with a specific example. Suppose the equilibrium price of cigarettes is initially $3 per pack. The government then imposes an excise tax of $2 per pack. What happens to the price of cigarettes?

The important point is that the price will not rise by the full $2 tax. Part of the **burden of the tax** will be paid by buyers. Part will be paid by sellers. Who **bears the burden** of the tax depends on how much quantity demanded and quantity supplied each respond to price increases.

Faced with a $2 per pack excise tax, sellers will initially want to raise the price of a pack of cigarettes by the full $2. But were they to do so, sales would fall as quantity demanded dropped. Sellers will be able to raise the price, but not by the full $2.

The burden of the tax does not matter who actuall[_] government. The seller can gather the tax from the buyer[_] government. Or the buyer can write a check to the govern[_] is easier if sellers remit the tax to the government. But r[_] mails the taxes to the government, the burden of the tax[_]

Figure 4.3a illustrates. The initial equilibrium price i[_] steep because smoking is addictive. Buyers respond to changes ɪɪɪ ᴘʀɪᴄᴄ. __ price rises, the drop in quantity demanded is relatively small.

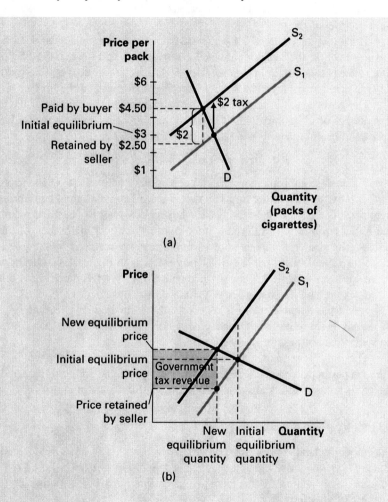

(a)

(b)

Figure 4.3 An excise tax.
A $2 per pack tax on cigarettes shifts the supply curve in Figure 4.3a up by $2. The equilibrium price rises to $4.50. The sellers remit $2 per pack to the government, so the price they retain is $2.50. The government tax revenue is equal to the shaded area in Figure 4.3b, which is the area of the rectangle whose base is the new equilibrium quantity and whose height is the tax.

$2 excise tax means that for each quantity, sellers want to receive $2 from buyers. Each quantity supplied on the initial supply curve, S_1, is now associated with a price $2 higher. The entire supply curve shifts up by $2, the size of the tax.

At a price of $5—the initial equilibrium price plus the excise tax—the quantity supplied exceeds the quantity demanded. Price will not rise that high. Instead, the price settles somewhere between the initial price and the initial price plus the tax.

In Figure 4.3a, the new equilibrium price is $4.50. The buyer pays an extra $1.50 per pack, three-fourths of the $2 tax. Economists say: The buyer is bearing three-fourths of the tax.

The seller receives $4.50 per pack from the buyer, but must send $2 to the government. So the net price the seller retains is $4.50 − $2.00 = $2.50 per pack. The seller is retaining 50 cents less per pack than before the tax, one-fourth of the $2 tax. Economists say: The seller is bearing one-fourth of the tax.

The government is receiving tax revenue equal to the amount of the tax times the number of units sold. This is equal to the area of a rectangle whose base is the new equilibrium quantity and whose height is the $2 tax.

Area of rectangle = base × height

Figure 4.3b shows a more general depiction of an excise tax. The supply curve shifts up by the size of the tax. The rise in price from the initial equilibrium to the new price is the burden of the tax for buyers. The fall in net price retained from the initial equilibrium to the new price minus the tax is the burden of the tax for sellers. The shaded rectangle shows the tax revenue received by the government.

When the demand curve is relatively steep as in Figure 4.3a, buyers pay more of the tax than do sellers. Quantity demanded does not fall much when price rises, so sellers are able to pass most of the tax on to consumers.

When the demand curve is relatively flat as in Figure 4.3b, sellers pay more of the tax than do buyers. Quantity demanded falls a great deal when price rises, so sellers cannot pass much of the tax on to consumers.

The only case in which consumers pay the entire tax is when the demand curve is perfectly vertical. Consumers pay any price and so in this rare and almost-never-seen case, sellers are able to pass the entire tax on to consumers.

Elasticity

We know demand curves slope down. When price rises, quantity demanded falls. But *by how much* does quantity demanded fall? Does it fall a little? A lot? How responsive is quantity demanded to changes in price? Economists call this the concept of **elasticity**.

Elasticity can be applied to anything. *How much* do polling numbers respond to negative political news? Elasticity. *How much* does an inflated balloon give without popping when you stand on it? Elasticity. *How much* does the rubber band stretch when you pull on it? Elasticity.

In economics, the most common application of elasticity is to quantity deman-ded. How much does quantity demanded rise when price falls? **Price elasticity of demand**. How much does quantity demanded rise when income rises? **Income**

elasticity of demand. How much does quantity of spiral notebooks demanded rise when pen prices rise? **Cross-price elasticity of demand**.

Economics focuses primarily on the price elasticity of demand. We know quantity demanded falls when price rises; demand curves slope down. But *by how much* does quantity demanded fall? The answer is the price elasticity of demand.

Price elasticity of demand is calculated as

$$\frac{\% \ change \ in \ quantity \ demanded}{\% \ change \ in \ price}$$

If quantity demanded rises by 5 percent when price falls by 10 percent, price elasticity of demand is $+5/-10 = -0.5$. If quantity demanded rises by 20 percent when price falls by 10 percent, price elasticity of demand is $+20/-10 = -2.0$.

Price elasticity of demand is always negative. This is because quantity demanded and price always move in opposite directions. Many people are less comfortable with negative numbers than they are with positive numbers. For this reason, some textbooks express the price elasticity of demand as a positive number. Rather than reporting a price elasticity of demand of -0.5, these books take the absolute value (ignore the minus sign) and report the value as 0.5. You need to look at your textbook to find out whether it reports price elasticity of demand as negative or positive numbers.

If quantity demanded does not change when price changes, price elasticity of demand equals zero. Economists call this **perfectly inelastic demand**. The demand curve would be completely vertical.

If quantity demanded drops to 0 when price rises even the smallest amount, price elasticity of demand approaches negative infinity. Economists call this **perfectly elastic demand**. The demand curve would be horizontal.

If the percentage change in quantity demanded is smaller than the percentage change in price (though in the opposite direction, of course), price elasticity of demand is between 0 and (negative) 1. Even a large drop in price results in only a small increase in quantity demanded. In this case, economists say: Demand is **inelastic**.

If the percentage change in quantity demanded is larger than the percentage change in price (though, again, in the opposite direction), price elasticity of demand is between (negative) 1 and (negative) infinity. A small drop in price results in a large increase in quantity demanded. Economists say: Demand is **elastic**.

In the rare case that the percentage change in quantity demanded equals the percentage change in price, demand is said to exhibit **unitary elasticity**.

TRY

In each case below, what is the value of the price elasticity of demand? Is demand perfectly inelastic, inelastic, unitarily elastic, elastic, or perfectly elastic?

5. When price falls by 10 percent, quantity demanded rises by 8 percent.

6. When price rises by 3 percent, quantity demanded falls by 3 percent.

7. When price rises by 1 percent, quantity demanded falls by 5 percent.

8. When price rises by 5 percent, quantity demanded collapses to zero.

9. When price falls by 2 percent, quantity demanded does not change.

Midpoint Method

The **midpoint method** is one method of calculating the percentage change. When price rises from $100 to $110, that is a 10 percent increase in price. But when price falls from $110 back to $100, that is only a 9.1 percent drop in price. Which value do we use: 10 percent or 9.1 percent?

There is no obvious answer to the question. One solution is to use the average of—the midpoint between—the two values. The formula for calculating the percentage change, using the midpoint method, is

$$\frac{\textit{difference between two values}}{\textit{average of two values}} = \frac{\textit{new value} - \textit{old value}}{\left(\textit{new value} + \textit{old value}\big/2\right)}$$

This midpoint method is then used to calculate both the percentage change in quantity demanded and the percentage change in price. The price elasticity of demand would then be calculated as

$$\frac{\% \textit{ change in quantity}}{\% \textit{ change in price}} = \frac{\dfrac{\textit{new quantity} - \textit{old quantity}}{\left(\textit{new quantity} + \textit{old quantity}\big/2\right)}}{\dfrac{\textit{new price} - \textit{old price}}{\left(\textit{new price} + \textit{old price}\big/2\right)}}$$

$$= \frac{\left(\dfrac{\textit{new quantity} - \textit{old quantity}}{\textit{new quantity} + \textit{old quantity}}\right)}{\left(\dfrac{\textit{new price} - \textit{old price}}{\textit{new price} + \textit{old price}}\right)}$$

Elasticity is an important concept. The midpoint method often bogs students down. If you can focus just on the definitions of elasticity in the previous section and overlook the material in this section, you will probably be much happier. That said, some instructors require students to calculate elasticities using the midpoint method.

TRY

In each case below, calculate the price elasticity of demand using the midpoint method.

10. When price rises from $5 to $6, quantity demanded falls from 100 to 95.

11. When price rises from $5 to $10, quantity demanded falls from 2,000 to 500.

12. When price falls from $8 to $7, quantity demanded rises from 10,000 to 11,000.

Total Revenue Effect

Total revenue is price times quantity. It is the total amount of money that sellers receive. When sellers increase price, does total revenue rise or fall or stay the same? The answer depends on the price elasticity of demand. Economists call this the **total revenue effect** of elasticity.

If demand is price inelastic, even a large increase in price will have little effect on quantity demanded. So an increase in price raises total revenue when demand is inelastic. A decrease in price lowers total revenue when demand is inelastic.

If demand is price elastic, even a small increase in price will have a big effect on quantity demanded. So an increase in price lowers total revenue when demand is elastic. A decrease in price raises total revenue when demand is elastic.

In the rare case that demand is unitarily elastic, the percentage change in price will be matched by the percentage change in quantity. An increase in price will have no effect on total revenue.

The total revenue effect is the most important application of elasticity. Should the bus company raise fares as a means of increasing revenue? Only if demand for bus transportation is price inelastic. Will a sale on breakfast cereal increase revenue from cereal sales? Only if demand for breakfast cereal is elastic. Of all the topics covered in this chapter, applications of elasticity are most likely to appear in day-to-day living.

TRY

In each case below, predict the impact on total revenue.

13. Demand for cigarettes is price inelastic. Cigarette sellers raise the price of cigarettes.

14. Demand for chocolate is price elastic. Chocolate sellers raise the price of chocolate.

15. Demand for recreational airline travel is price elastic. Airlines cut the price of tickets to Orlando, Florida, the home of DisneyWorld.

CONSUMER AND PRODUCER SURPLUS

Consumer Surplus

When a market reaches equilibrium, there is one price charged to all buyers. But some buyers are willing to pay a much higher price than the equilibrium price. Economists say these buyers are receiving **consumer surplus**. The consumer surplus is the difference between the price buyers are willing and able to pay, and the price actually paid.

TIP

Consumer surplus is in no way connected with the concept of market surplus, the difference between quantity supplied and quantity demanded when price is above the equilibrium price.

You find a pen you like and are willing to pay $3.00 for it. The price is just $2.00. Hooray! You are enjoying a consumer surplus of $1.00 because you paid one dollar less than the maximum you were willing to pay.

The market consumer surplus is just the sum of all the individual buyers' consumer surpluses. When there are many buyers, the value of consumer surplus is determined with a graph.

The market for pens depicted in Figure 4.4a has an equilibrium price of $2.00. The equilibrium quantity is 8,000 pens. The consumer surplus is the area below the demand curve and above the equilibrium price. The area of a triangle is found by the formula

$$area\ of\ a\ triangle = \tfrac{1}{2} \times base \times height$$

The base of the triangle is 8,000 units. The height is $3.00, which is the distance between the equilibrium price and the price where the demand curve touches the vertical axis. So the consumer surplus in the market for pens is

$$consumer\ surplus = \tfrac{1}{2} \times equilibrium\ quantity$$
$$\times (maximum\ demand\ price - equilibrium\ price)$$
$$consumer\ surplus = \tfrac{1}{2} \times 8,000\ pens \times \$3.00\ per\ pen = \$12,000$$

In general, the value of the consumer surplus is equal to the area below the demand curve and above the equilibrium price, as shown in Figure 4.4b. Any

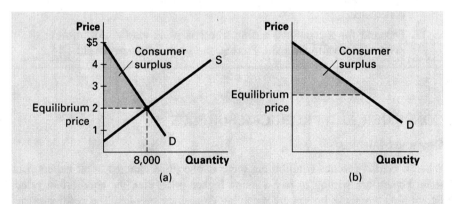

Figure 4.4 Consumer surplus.
The consumer surplus is equal to the area below the demand curve and above the equilibrium price, as shown in Figure 4.4b. In Figure 4.4a, the size of the consumer surplus is 1/2 × 8,000 × $3 = $12,000.

time the demand curve is downward sloping rather than horizontal, the market will generate some consumer surplus. Some buyers will be able to pay less for the item than the maximum they are willing to pay.

Producer Surplus

Producers (sellers) also enjoy a surplus. For many producers, the market equilibrium price is above the minimum price they are willing to accept. Economists say these producers are receiving **producer surplus**. The producer surplus is the difference between the minimum price sellers are willing to accept and the price they actually receive.

TIP

There is no connection between the concepts of producer surplus and market surplus.

Harry's Office Supply Store is willing to sell you a pen for $1.50. But the market price is $2.00 so Harry's charges $2.00 per pen. Hooray for Harry! He is enjoying a producer surplus of $0.50 because he received 50 cents more for the pen than the minimum he was willing to accept.

The market producer surplus is just the sum of all the individual sellers' producer surpluses. When there are many sellers, the value of producer surplus is determined with a graph.

The market for pens is depicted in Figure 4.5a, which is a repeat of Figure 4.4a. The equilibrium price is $2.00 and equilibrium quantity is 8,000 pens. The producer

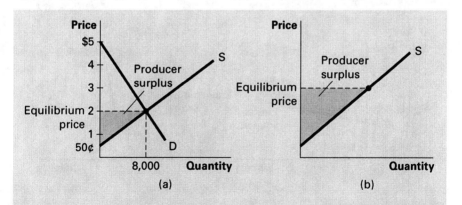

Figure 4.5 Producer surplus.
The producer surplus is equal to the area above the supply curve and below the equilirium price, as shown in Figure 4.5b. In Figure 4.5a, the producer surplus is equal to $1/2 \times 8,000 \times \$1.50 = \$6,000$.

surplus is the area above the supply curve and below the price. In this case,

producer surplus = $^{1}/_{2}$ × *equilibrium quantity*

× *(equilibrium price − minimum supply price)*

producer surplus = $^{1}/_{2}$ × 8,000 *pens* × ($2.00 − $0.50) *per pen* = $6,000

In general, the value of the producer surplus is equal to the area above the supply curve and below the equilibrium price, as shown in Figure 4.5b. Anytime the supply curve is upward sloping rather than horizontal, the market will generate some producer surplus. Some sellers will receive more for the good than the minimum they are willing to accept.

Surplus and Elasticity

The slopes of the supply and demand curves determine how much surplus producers and consumers receive. When demand is very price elastic—a small change in price results in a large change in quantity demanded—consumers receive very little consumer surplus. See Figure 4.6a. There is little difference in this case between the equilibrium price and the maximum price consumers are willing to pay.

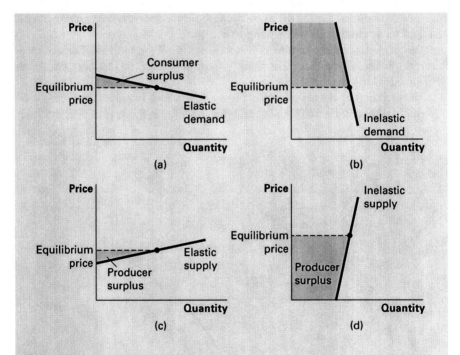

Figure 4.6 Surplus and elasticity.

When demand is elastic, consumer surplus is relatively small. When demand is inelastic, consumer surplus is relatively large. When supply is elastic, producer surplus is relatively small. When supply is inelastic, producer surplus is relatively large.

When demand is very price inelastic as in Figure 4.6b—even a large change in price has a small effect on quantity demanded—consumers receive a lot of consumer surplus. Many, many consumers are able to buy the product at a price far lower than the maximum they are willing to pay.

When supply is very price elastic as in Figure 4.6c, a small change in price has a large effect on quantity supplied. Producers receive very little producer surplus because there is little difference between the equilibrium price and the minimum price producers are willing to accept.

When supply is very price inelastic as in Figure 4.6d, even a large change in price results in very little change in quantity supplied. Producers receive a great deal of producer surplus because there is a big difference between the equilibrium price and the minimum price sellers are willing to accept.

DEADWEIGHT LOSS OF A TAX

Markets maximize **total surplus**, the sum of consumer surplus (CS) and producer surplus (PS). Price floors result in a loss of quantity sold and lower surplus. Price ceilings do the same. Economists call the loss of surplus a **deadweight loss**.

The most common illustration of deadweight loss (DWL) is in the case of an excise tax. Remember: An excise tax causes the equilibrium price to rise and equilibrium quantity to fall. The higher equilibrium price lowers consumer surplus because there is a smaller gap between the maximum price some buyers are willing to pay and the price they actually pay. Not only that, the lower equilibrium quantity lowers consumer surplus because fewer people are buying the product.

The excise tax is borne by both the buyers and the sellers. The equilibrium price rises but not by the full amount of the tax. So the price retained by the seller—the difference between the new equilibrium price and the excise tax—falls below the initial equilibrium price. Producer surplus falls. Not only that, the lower equilibrium quantity lowers producer surplus because fewer sellers are selling the product.

Not all of the lost consumer and producer surplus is completely gone. The government receives increased revenue from the excise tax equal to the tax times the equilibrium quantity.

The **deadweight loss of the tax** is the initial total surplus minus the sum of the final total surplus and the government revenue.

DWL = initial CS + initial PS − (new CS + new PS + government revenue)

Figure 4.7 illustrates the deadweight loss of a tax.

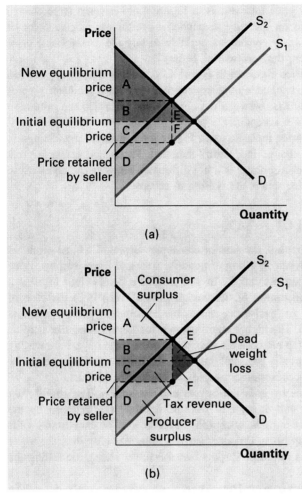

(a)

(b)

Figure 4.7 Deadweight loss of a tax.

Before the imposition of the tax, consumer surplus is the dark shaded area in Figure 4.7a, equal to the sum of areas A + B + E. The initial producer surplus is the light shaded area, equal to the sum of areas C + D + F. The tax lowers consumer surplus to the area A in Figure 4.7b. The tax lowers producer surplus to the shaded area D. The government collects tax revenue equal to the sum of areas B + C. The deadweight loss of the tax is equal to the sum of areas E + F.

Chapter 5

Consumer Theory

Why does the demand curve slope down? You may think it's intuitive: When something becomes more expensive, you buy less of it. Movie theater ticket prices go up, you go to the movies less often. Economists explain this inverse relationship between prices and quantity demanded with the concepts of utility and indifference curves. In this chapter, we also look at the income and substitution effects of a change in price.

KEY TERMS AND CONCEPTS

- Utility
- Utils
- Interpersonal comparison of utils
- Total utility
- Marginal utility
- Law of diminishing marginal utility
- Maximize utility
- Utility maximization rule
- Budget constraint
- Budget line
- Slope of the budget line
- Indifferent
- Indifference curve
- Convex to the origin
- Slope of the indifference curve
- Marginal rate of substitution
- Diminishing marginal rate of substitution
- Tangent
- Income effect
- Substitution effect

KEY EQUATIONS

- Marginal utility
- Utility maximization rule

- Budget constraint
- Marginal rate of substitution

KEY GRAPHS

- Budget constraint
- Indifference curve

UTILITY MAXIMIZATION

Why do we buy things? Because these things give us satisfaction. Maybe the form of that satisfaction is survival. Maybe it is meeting obligations. Maybe it is doing for others. Maybe it is joy. Satisfaction comes in many forms. But generally, we buy things not because we are forced to (even buying a required textbook is ultimately a decision left to us) but because we want to. Economists say: We buy things because they give us **utility**.

Utility is satisfaction. Some people think utility is greed, but it need not be so. Whatever gives you satisfaction, whatever gives you happiness, those things give you utility. Paying your rent so you have a place to sleep gives you utility. Buying food so you are not hungry gives you utility. Buying a required textbook so you can earn a higher grade gives you utility. Giving money to the Red Cross for disaster relief because you want to help others gives you utility. Utility is simply the economist's word for satisfaction.

Economists like to count and measure, so they pretend that we can count utility. The units of utility are called **utils**. This is all make-believe. How satisfied or happy do you feel when you pay your rent? "Pretty good. It's better than sleeping on the street," you say. Economists pretend you can put a number on that feeling: "I get 400 utils of satisfaction from paying my rent."

You and I can't compare how many utils of satisfaction we each get from paying our rent. You can compare your utility from paying your rent with your utility from buying food. I can compare my utility from paying my rent with my utility from buying food. But you can't compare your utility from paying your rent with my utility from paying my rent. It's all make-believe, anyway. So you can rank your feelings—shelter is better than food, food is better than clothing, clothing is better than chocolate. But you can't say who gets more satisfaction from paying their rent: you or me. Economists say: There is no **interpersonal comparison of utils**.

The more you consume of one particular item, the more utility you receive. If one apple is good, two are better. If two are good, three apples are better still. Economists say: Your **total utility** rises as you consume a greater quantity of any one item.

The additional utility you receive from each additional apple is the **marginal utility** of that apple. The first apple gave you 50 utils of satisfaction. The second apple gave you 40 utils. The third apple gave you 25 utils. Your total utility from buying all three apples is $50 + 40 + 25 = 115$ utils. The marginal utility of the second apple is 40 utils. The marginal utility of the third apple is 25 utils.

Marginal utility is the change in total utility from consuming one more unit of an item.

Marginal utility of consuming n^{th} unit = Total utility from consuming n units
                                              $-$ total utility from consuming $n - 1$ units

Your total utility of consuming 2 pounds of beef is (let's pretend) 1,800 utils. Your total utility of consuming 3 pounds of beef is 2,025 utils. So your additional utility from consuming the third pound of beef is the difference, 2,025 $-$ 1,800 utils, or 225 utils. Economists would say: The marginal utility of consuming the third pound of beef is 225 utils.

Because more is better—an assumption economists make—total utility always increases as the quantity of an item increases. The additional utility you receive from each additional unit of an item must therefore always be positive. Economists say: Marginal utility is always positive.

More is better, but more and more and more is only a bit better. The additional utility we get from an additional unit of an item gets smaller and smaller and smaller as we consume more and more and more. The marginal utility diminishes —decreases—as quantity rises. Economists call this the **law of diminishing marginal utility**. A law, remember, is something that is nearly always true.

TRY

Answers to all "TRY" problems are in the back of the book.

  1. You derive 100 utils of total satisfaction from spending 1 hour helping your grandmother, and 180 utils of total satisfaction from spending 2 hours helping her. What is your marginal utility of the first hour of helping Grandma? Of the second hour of helping her?

Economists often show total utility and marginal utility with a graph. Figure 5.1a shows your total utility from consuming apples. Eat one apple and your total utility (*TU*) is 50 utils. Eat two apples and your *TU* is 90 utils. Eat three apples and your *TU* is 115 utils. Total utility increases as the number of apples consumed increases.

Marginal utility is the additional utility from consuming one more apple. Figure 5.1b shows your marginal utility from consuming apples. The marginal utility (*MU*) of the first apple is 50 utils. The marginal utility of the second apple is 40 utils. The *MU* of the third apple is 25 utils.

The marginal utility curve in Figure 5.1b is above the horizontal axis. That's because marginal utility is always positive. But marginal utility diminishes—gets smaller—as more apples are consumed. So the marginal utility curve slopes down.

Beef also gives you utility. Table 5.1 shows the total utility and marginal utility you derive from consuming (buying) apples and beef. We will call apples "A" and beef "B."

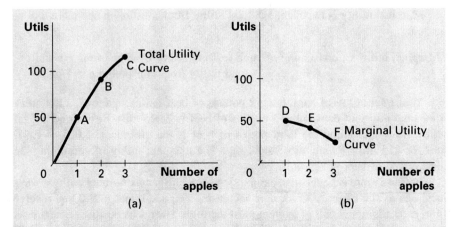

Figure 5.1 Total utility and marginal utility curves.

The total utility curve in Figure 5.1a shows how total utility rises as consumption of apples rises. Total utility (TU) of consuming one apple is 50 utils (point A). The TU of consuming two apples is 90 utils (point B). The TU of consuming three apples is 115 utils (point C). The marginal utility curve in Figure 5.1b shows the additional utility from consuming one more apple. The marginal utility (MU) of the first apple is 50 utils (point D). The MU of the second apple is 40 utils (point E). The MU of the third apple is 25 utils (point F).

Marginal utility declines—diminishes—as quantity increases. You can probably think of exceptions, but doing so won't help you learn this material. There are plenty of examples that confirm the law of diminishing marginal utility. When you eat at an all-you-can-eat restaurant (or dining commons), do you eventually stop eating? Yes, of course. Why? Because one more helping and your pants will split. The satisfaction from the next trip to the serving counter is not sufficient to make you get up out of your seat and go get the food.

When you buy a newspaper out of a rack on the street corner, do you take just one paper even though you could just as easily grab several? Yes. Why? Because a second newspaper doesn't give you as much satisfaction as the first.

When you find a pair of jeans that fit right and look good, do you buy dozens of pairs? No. Why not? Because you like having some variety in your wardrobe, so the 12th identical pair of jeans does not give you as much satisfaction as the first.

Table 5.1 Total and Marginal Utilities from Apples and Beef

Quantity of apples (Q_A)	Total utility from apples	Marginal utility of that apple (MU_A)	Quantity (pounds) of beef (Q_B)	Total utility from beef	Marginal utility of that pound of beef (MU_B)
1	50	50	1	1,000	1,000
2	90	40	2	1,800	800
3	115	25	3	2,025	225
4	137	22	4	2,125	100
5	158	21	5	2,175	50

Utility Maximization

Our goal as consumers, economists assume, is to spend our income so as to get as much utility as possible. Economists say: Assume consumers wish to **maximize utility**. What do we buy to maximize utility? How many of which goods do we buy to give ourselves the most satisfaction?

The answer depends on the prices of what we buy. The *utility* we derive from apples does not depend on how much we pay for apples. Free, expensive, or some place in between—the satisfaction you derive from the first apple is 50 utils. Utility doesn't depend on price, but how many apples we buy *does* depend on how much we pay for apples.

You have $20 to spend. Beef costs $5 per pound. Apples cost $1 each. How do you spend your money? To maximize utility, each dollar spent should bring you the greatest possible additional satisfaction.

Take a look at Table 5.1. Your first $5 is spent on a pound of beef, garnering you 1,000 utils of satisfaction, which is $1,000/5 = 200$ utils of satisfaction per dollar. Your next $5 is spent on a second pound of beef, whose marginal utility is 800 utils, or 160 utils per dollar. So far you have spent $10 and received 1,800 utils of satisfaction.

Now what? You could spend $5 on a third pound of beef, which would give you 225 utils of satisfaction, or $225/5 = 45$ utils per dollar. Or you could buy one apple for $1, which would give you 50 utils of satisfaction, or 50 utils per dollar. Buy the apple. You are a utility maximizer. Buying the apple next for $1 will give you more utility than using that $1 to buy 1/5 of a third pound of beef.

Do you see what we're doing? Each time we have to decide how to spend the next dollar, we look to see which good gives us the most satisfaction for that dollar. We're allocating our money one dollar at a time. Do you and I really behave this way? Not exactly ... but sort of. When you've got just $20 left in your wallet and your checking account is empty, how will you spend that $20? You'll buy the things that give you the most satisfaction for that $20. Economists say: You will allocate your income so as to maximize your utility.

You've spent $11 so far. What's next? Buy the third pound of beef for $5 because it gives you 225 utils of satisfaction, 45 utils per dollar. Now you have spent $16.

And now what? Buy four more apples. Each apple gives you more additional utility than would the fourth pound of beef. You have spent your $20 on 3 pounds of beef and 5 apples.

What is the rule we were following? Allocate your spending so that you get the greatest marginal utility per dollar with each dollar you spend. This follows the **utility maximization rule**: Consumers maximize utility if they allocate their spending so that, with their last dollar spent, the marginal utility *per dollar* of each item purchased is the same. Consumers maximize utility when, as they spend their last dollar,

$$\frac{MU_A}{P_A} = \frac{MU_B}{P_B} = \frac{MU_C}{P_C}$$

where A, B, and C represent all of the items purchased (e.g., apples, beef, and carrots).

The utility maximization rule doesn't work exactly for small quantities like we have in Table 5.1. But it comes close. For larger quantities and larger amounts of money, this rule works. Spend our income so that as we spend our last dollar, the marginal utility per dollar (*MU* divided by Price) is the same for each and every thing we buy, and we will have maximized our utility.

TRY

2. What is the utility maximization rule?
3. The table below shows the total utility from buying jicama, kettle corn, and licorice. Jicama costs $2 each. Kettle corn costs $3 each. Licorice costs $1 each. Fill in the *MU/P* columns. You have $15 to spend. What is the utility maximizing combination of jicama, kettle corn, and licorice you'll purchase?

Jicama ($2 each)			Kettle corn ($3 each)			Licorice ($1 each)		
Quantity (Q_J)	Total utility (TU_J)	Marginal utility per dollar (MU_J/P_J)	Quantity (Q_K)	Total utility (TU_K)	Marginal utility per dollar (MU_K/P_K)	Quantity (Q_L)	Total utility (TU_L)	Marginal utility per dollar (MU_L/P_L)
1	80		1	180		1	80	
2	120		2	330		2	140	
3	140		3	420		3	185	
4	150		4	480		4	210	
5	156		5	510		5	230	

Demand Curves Slope Down

The utility maximization rule coupled with the law of diminishing marginal utility explains why demand curves slope down.

What if the price of apples rises? Nothing happens to the satisfaction we derive from consuming apples. Our marginal utilities remain the same. But the marginal utility *per dollar* falls when the price rises. If we don't change the quantities we are buying, then marginal utility per dollar will no longer be equal for all goods. *MU/P* will be less for apples than it is for other goods.

If we are to maximize utility, we must reallocate our spending so that once again the marginal utility per dollar of the last dollar spent is the same for all goods. How can we change our spending in order to once again make *MU/P* the same for all goods?

Here is where the law of diminishing marginal utility comes in. We know that marginal utility diminishes (falls) as the quantity consumed rises. Go in the opposite direction: Marginal utility will rise as the quantity consumed falls. If you buy fewer apples, you'll increase the marginal utility per dollar (*MU/P*) you receive from the last apple. That's the way to once again make *MU/P* equal for all goods! Buy fewer apples when they become more expensive.

The logic goes like this: As the price of an item rises, its marginal utility per dollar falls. *MU/P* for the now-pricier item is now less than *MU/P* for everything else. We will change our spending—economists say: we reallocate our budget—so the *MU/P* for that now-pricier item rises. To raise the marginal utility, we consume less of that item. Quantity demanded falls.

We consume less because of the law of diminishing marginal utility: buy less and our marginal utility from the last unit purchased will rise. Higher price, consume less, higher marginal utility . . .   all of the marginal utilities per dollar will again be equal.

TRY

4. When apples cost $1 and beef costs $5 per pound, the utility-maximizing way to spend $20 was to buy 3 pounds of beef and 5 apples. If the price of apples increases to $1.50, how many apples and how much beef will you buy if you have $20 to spend? (You can buy parts of a pound of beef.)

Quantity of apples (Q_A)	Total utility from apples	Marginal utility per dollar when $P_A = \$1$ ($MU_A/\$1$)	Marginal utility per dollar when $P_A = \$1.50$ ($MU_A/\$1.50$)	Quantity (pounds) of beef (Q_B)	Total utility from beef	Marginal utility per dollar when $P_B = \$5$ ($MU_B/\$5$)
1	50	50		1	1,000	200
2	90	40		2	1,800	160
3	115	25		3	2,025	45
4	137	22		4	2,125	20
5	158	21		5	2,175	10

BUDGET CONSTRAINT

You can't always get what you want. We are constrained by our budgets. Whether we are only spending our current income, or spending our income plus some savings, or spending our income plus borrowing, there is some total budget that binds or constrains our spending. Economists say: We face a **budget constraint**.

Suppose your total budget, the total you can spend in a month, is $1,000. How you spend your $1,000 depends on the prices of what you buy and how much you buy. If apples are $1 each, you could buy 1,000 apples ... but nothing else. If beef is $5 per pound, you could buy 200 pounds of beef ... but nothing else. If carrots are $2 a pound, you could buy 500 pounds of carrots ... but nothing else. Or you could buy all sorts of combinations of apples, beef, and carrots, so long as the total you spent is no more than $1,000.

We can put all this information into one equation, using P to stand for price and Q to stand for quantity:

$$P_A \times Q_A + P_B \times Q_B + P_C \times Q_C \leq \text{Total budget}$$

or in our example,

$$\$1 \times Q_{\text{apples}} + \$5 \times Q_{\text{beef}} + \$2 \times Q_{\text{carrots}} \leq \$1,000$$

that is,

$$\$1 \times \text{Quantity of apples} + \$5 \times \text{Quantity of beef}$$
$$+ \$2 \times \text{Quantity of carrots} \leq \$1,000$$

You could buy 100 apples, 100 pounds of beef, and 200 pounds of carrots. Or, you could buy 250 apples, 110 pounds of beef, and 100 pounds of carrots. Many other combinations are also possible.

If there are just two items that we can purchase, the budget constraint can be graphed. Apples (A) and beef (B) are the only two items. The total budget is $1,000. Apples cost $1 each. Beef costs $5 per pound.

On the vertical axis, we show the number of apples (Q_A) that can be purchased. The vertical intercept is the maximum number of apples you can buy. The maximum is the total budget divided by the price of apples: $1,000/\$1 = 1,000$ apples. The vertical intercept is 1,000 apples.

On the horizontal axis, we show the number of pounds of beef (Q_B) that can be purchased. The maximum amount of beef you could buy is $1,000/\$5 = 200$ pounds of beef. The horizontal intercept is 200 pounds of beef.

A straight line connects these two points, as seen in Figure 5.2a. Any combination of apples and beef that falls on or to the left of the line is affordable. Any combination that is on the line uses the entire budget. Economists call this line the **budget line**.

The **slope of the budget line** is the ratio of the prices. Remember that slope is rise over run. Use the two intercepts to determine the slope. The rise, the vertical intercept, is the total budget divided by the price of apples: budget/P_A. The run, the negative (or, opposite) of the horizontal intercept, is the negative of the total

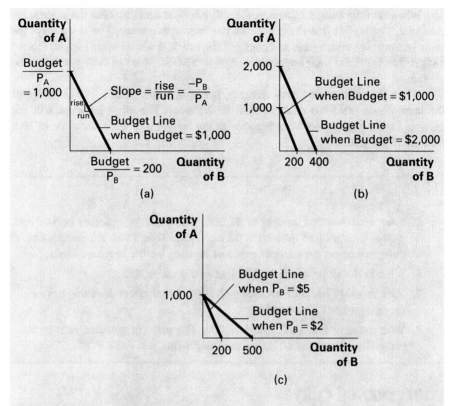

Figure 5.2 Budget lines.

The budget line shows the combinations of goods A and B that the consumer can afford to purchase. The slope of the budget line is $-P_B/P_A$. In Figure 5.2b, the budget line shifts out as the total budget increases from \$1,000 to \$2,000. In Figure 5.2c, the budget line pivots as the price of good B changes from \$5 to \$2.

budget divided by the price of beef: $-\frac{\text{budget}}{P_B}$. The slope of the budget line is

$$\text{slope of budget line} = \frac{\text{rise}}{\text{run}} = \frac{\text{budget}/P_A}{-\text{budget}/P_B} = -\frac{P_B}{P_A} \; \dot{=} \; -\frac{P_x}{P_y}$$

The slope of the budget line is the negative of the ratio of the price of the item measured on the horizontal axis to the price of the item measured on the vertical axis.

TIP

Don't lose that minus sign! The budget line slopes down. So its slope is negative.

When the total budget increases, the entire budget line shifts but the slope stays the same. The budget line shifts because the intercepts change. The slope stays the same because the prices have not changed. Figure 5.2b shows what happens to the budget line when the total budget increases to $2,000. More of both goods can be purchased.

When the price of one item changes, the budget line pivots. The intercept of the item whose price has changed will be different. The other intercept will not change. Figure 5.2c shows what happens to the budget line when the price of beef falls to $2 per pound.

TRY

5. Your total monthly budget is $2,000. The price of gasoline is $4 per gallon. The price of housing is $2 per square foot. Draw the budget line. Put gasoline on the vertical axis and housing on the horizontal axis.

6. What is the slope of the budget line you drew in #5?

7. Your monthly budget increases to $3,000. What effect does this have on the budget line? On its slope?

8. Your monthly budget is again $2,000. The price of gasoline falls to $2 per gallon. Show the effect on the budget line you drew in #5.

INDIFFERENCE CURVES

Utility analysis is one way to explain why demand curves slope down. Another way is with indifference curves. They are based on the same notion that people derive utility from consuming goods and services, and that the marginal utility from each additional unit declines as we consume more and more of any particular item. Total spending is limited by the budget constraint.

TIP

Some instructors do not discuss indifference curves in Principles classes. Check your syllabus and your textbook.

A key assumption is that there are only two goods that we can consume, say A (apples) and B (beef). The question is: For you, an individual consumer, what are the various combinations of apples and beef that will yield for you the *same amount of utility*? Perhaps 100 apples and 50 pounds of beef give you total utility of 1,000 utils. If instead you consumed only 80 apples, how many pounds of beef would you need to consume to still receive 1,000 utils of satisfaction from apples and beef? Surely you would need to consume more than 50 pounds of beef in this case. Maybe 80 apples and 60 pounds of beef give you 1,000 utils of satisfaction.

What if you consumed 120 apples? Then perhaps it would be 45 pounds of beef and 120 apples for 1,000 utils of satisfaction.

Which of these three combinations of apples and beef do you prefer? You don't. You are equally happy with each of these combinations. Why? Because each combination gives you the same amount of utility. Economists say: You are **indifferent** between any of these possible combinations of apples and beef, because they all give you the same amount of utility.

Indifference curves are, no surprise, curves. This analysis is presented with graphs. Draw a graph that shows all of the possible combinations of apples and beef that give you 1,000 utils of satisfaction. Economists call that curve an **indifference curve**.

The indifference curve will look like the curve in Figure 5.3a. It slopes down because to keep total utility constant, more beef (B) will be offset by fewer apples (A). The indifference curve is not a straight line because of the law of diminishing marginal utility. If you are not consuming much beef, then you're willing to give up many apples to gain a little bit of beef. But if you are already consuming a lot of beef, you won't give up many apples at all to gain more beef because yet more beef gives you very little additional satisfaction. Economists describe the shape of the curves by saying: Indifference curves are **convex to the origin**.

The **slope of the indifference curve** depends on the marginal utilities of apples and beef. The slope changes as you move along the indifference curve. Figure 5.3a shows the slope. Remember: Total utility is constant along any

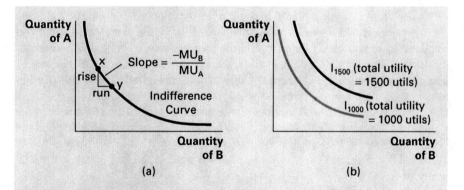

(a)   (b)

Figure 5.3 Indifference curves.

An indifference curve such as the one shown in Figure 5.3a shows the many combinations of goods A and B that each provide the same total utility. The indifference curve is downward sloping because more B is offset by less of A. It is convex to the origin because of the law of diminishing marginal utility. The slope of the indifference curve is $-MU_B/MU_A$, which economists call the marginal rate of substitution. The indifference curve labeled I_{1000} in Figure 5.3b shows the combination of goods A and B that provide total utility of 1,000 utils. Combinations of goods A and B that provide more utility are further from the origin. The indifference curve I_{1500} shows combinations of A and B that provide 1,500 utils of satisfaction.

indifference curve. When you move between points x and y, total utility does not change. You lose utility equal to $\Delta Q_A \times MU_A$. (Remember: MU_A is the change in utility from consuming *one* more unit of A.) You gain utility equal to $\Delta Q_B \times MU_B$. Total utility does not change, so the lost utility plus gained utility must equal zero.

$$\Delta Q_A \times MU_A + \Delta Q_B \times MU_B = 0$$

Manipulating

$$\Delta Q_A \times MU_A = -\Delta Q_B \times MU_B$$

Dividing

$$\frac{\Delta Q_A}{\Delta Q_B} = -\frac{MU_B}{MU_A}$$

ΔQ_A is the "rise" and ΔQ_B is the "run." So $\Delta Q_A / \Delta Q_B$ is the slope of the indifference curve.

$$\text{slope} = \frac{\text{rise}}{\text{run}} = \frac{\Delta Q_A}{\Delta Q_B} = -\frac{MU_B}{MU_A}$$

The slope of the indifference curve is the negative of the ratios of the marginal utilities of the two items. The slope measures the rate at which we substitute beef (measured on the horizontal axis) for apples (measured on the vertical axis). Economists say: The slope of the indifference curve is the **marginal rate of substitution**.

As we move along an indifference curve from upper left to lower right, the curve gets flatter and flatter. Ignoring the negative sign, the slope gets smaller and smaller (closer and closer to zero). The indifference curve gets flatter because of the law of diminishing marginal utility. Economists say: Because of the law of diminishing marginal utility, there is a **diminishing marginal rate of substitution** as we substitute more and more B for A.

Indifference curves with more of both apples and beef will be further from the origin. The further the indifference curve is from the origin, the higher the total utility. In Figure 5.3b we see two indifference curves. One is for total utility of 1,000 utils. The second curve, above and to the right of the first curve, is for total utility of 1,500 utils.

TRY

9. You derive 500 utils of satisfaction if you consume 150 gallons of gasoline and 600 square feet of housing in one month. You also derive 500 utils of satisfaction if you consume 100 gallons of gasoline and 900 square feet of housing in one month. Draw an indifference curve from this information. Label it I_{500}. Sketch in a second indifference curve for combinations of gasoline and housing that provide you with 800 utils of satisfaction.

10. What is the slope of an indifference curve between any two points?

11. Is the slope of an indifference curve the same all the way along the curve, or does the slope change as you move along an indifference curve?

12. Why is an indifference curve convex to the origin and not just a straight line?

CONSUMER EQUILIBRIUM AND THE DEMAND CURVE

Indifference curves are a second way to explain why demand curves slope down. We combine the budget constraint and the indifference curve on one graph. Consumers, we assume, want the highest level of utility possible. That means consumers want to be on the indifference curve that is furthest from the origin.

Consumers are, at the same time, constrained by their budget. So the combination of goods purchased must fall on the budget line.

Figure 5.4 illustrates. This consumer can afford to purchase any combination of apples (A) and beef (B) that is on or to the left of the budget line. So the combination represented by point 1, A_1 apples and B_1 pounds of beef, *can* be purchased. But this is not the highest possible level of utility.

The highest possible level of utility is represented by point 2, A_2 apples and B_2 pounds of beef. At point 2, consuming A_2 apples and B_2 pounds of beef, the

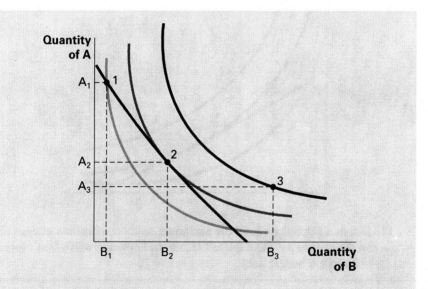

Figure 5.4 Maximizing utility.

A utility-maximizing consumer will purchase A_2 of good A and B_2 of good B, where the budget line is tangent to the indifference curve that is furthest from the origin. Combination 1 is affordable but does not maximize utility. Combination 3 is unaffordable.

consumer is on the budget line, so the combination is affordable. Point 3, which represents A_3 apples and B_3 pounds of beef, provides more utility, but because it is to the right of the budget line, it is unaffordable. The best the consumer can do—maximizing utility while satisfying the budget constraint—is to consume at point 2, A_2 apples and B_2 pounds of beef. At this point, the budget constraint is just **tangent** to the indifference curve.

TRY

13. Look at the graph below. Label each of the points marked in the graph with one of these four letters:

   A. The affordable combination of G and H that maximizes utility
   B. A combination of G and H that is affordable but doesn't maximize utility
   C. A combination of G and H that is unaffordable and provides less than the maximum utility
   D. A combination of G and H that is unaffordable but provides the same amount of utility as point "A"

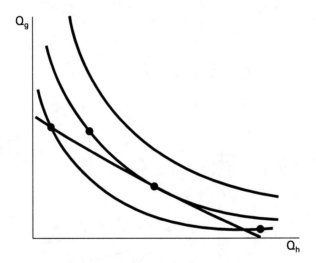

14. Sketch a graph that shows the maximum utility combination of eggs (E, on the vertical axis) and falafels (F, on the horizontal axis). Don't forget to include a budget line!

___

A demand curve shows how quantity demanded changes when price changes. Economists use indifference curves to explain why demand curves slope down. Remember: Demand curves slope down because when price falls, quantity demanded rises.

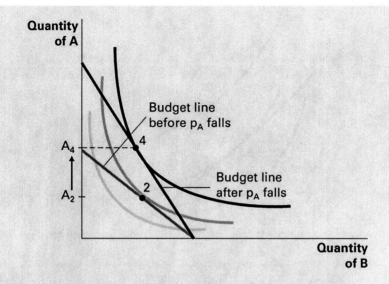

Figure 5.5 Quantity demanded changes when price changes.

When the price of good A falls, the budget line pivots. The utility-maximizing consumer will now purchase A_4 rather than just A_2 of good A. As the price of good A falls, the quantity demanded of A rises.

What is the quantity demanded of apples? Remember: Quantity demanded is the amount consumers are willing and able to purchase *at a particular price*. The budget constraint is drawn for a particular price of apples. The indifference curves are all about utility. Indifference curves do not change when price changes.

Figure 5.5 shows what happens when the price of apples rises. At the initial price of apples, we saw in Figure 5.4 that A_2 was the quantity of apples demanded. That point is shown in Figure 5.5 and again labeled "2".

The price of apples falls. What happens? When the price of apples falls, the budget constraint pivots up. The lower price of apples allows the consumer to buy more apples, moving to a higher indifference curve. The new quantity of apples demanded after the price of apples falls is A_4. At a lower price, a greater quantity is demanded. The demand curve slopes down.

TRY

15. In the graph on page 74, point "A" shows the utility-maximizing combination of gasoline and housing that you can buy, given the budget constraint. When the price of gasoline increases, what happens to the budget line? Sketch in a new budget line. Show what happens to the quantity of gasoline demanded. Does the demand curve for gasoline slope down?

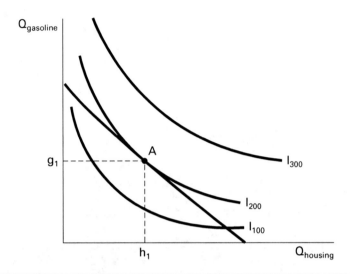

INCOME AND SUBSTITUTION EFFECTS

Two forces cause us to buy more of an item when its price falls. When the price of an item falls, we can buy more of everything. Our income goes further. So, a drop in the price of an item causes us to buy more of that item because we can afford to do so. Economists say: This is the **income effect** of a price change.

A second force reinforces the first. When the price of an item falls, we will substitute that now less expensive item for other goods and services. So, a drop in the price of an item causes us to buy more of that item because we substitute it for other items whose price has not fallen. Economists say: This is the **substitution effect** of a price change.

Both effects, the income effect and the substitution effect, take us to the same conclusion. Demand curves slope down. When the price of an item falls, our quantity demanded of that item rises.

CONCLUSION

Consumer theory is, for many students, some of the most difficult material in microeconomics. Some instructors skip the chapter entirely in a Principles course. Remember the point of it all: Demand curves slope down.

Chapter **6**

Perfectly Competitive Firms

Why does the supply curve slope up? Sellers increase quantity supplied when price rises. But why? The answer has everything to do with how firms maximize profit. In this chapter, we look at production and costs, and how perfectly competitive firms determine how much output to produce. We consider decisions that firms make in both the short run (when capital is fixed) and the long run (when capital can be varied).

KEY TERMS AND CONCEPTS

- Diminishing marginal returns
- Marginal cost
- Profit
- Maximize profit
- Costs
- Production
- Short run
- Capital
- Long run
- Fixed capital
- Variable inputs
- Marginal product
- Total product
- Production function
- Total cost
- Fixed costs
- Variable costs
- Marginal cost curve
- Average variable costs
- Average fixed costs
- Scale of production
- Long-run average total cost curve
- Constant returns to scale
- Economies of scale
- Increasing returns to scale

- Diseconomies of scale
- Decreasing returns to scale
- Profit-maximizing condition
- Perfect competition
- Monopoly
- Monopolistic competition
- Oligopoly
- Imperfect competition
- Price takers
- Revenue
- Marginal revenue
- Accounting profit
- Economic profit
- Normal rate of return on capital
- Abnormal profit
- Economic loss
- Normal profit
- Exit
- Shut-down point

KEY EQUATIONS

- Average total cost
- Total profit
- Profit-maximizing condition

KEY GRAPHS

- Long-run average total cost curve
- Profit maximization by the perfectly competitive firm
- Shut-down point

PRODUCTION AND PROFIT MAXIMIZATION

When firms try to produce more output, they need to hire more inputs. If there are only three machines that the workers can share, then the more workers the firm hires, the more crowded it will be around those three machines. In a store with 15 clerks and only three cash registers, clerks spend more time waiting for a free machine than in a store with only six clerks and three cash registers. Adding additional workers might not help so much—might not add very much output—once the machines are all busy. Economists say: Firms encounter **diminishing marginal returns** as they increase the quantity of one input (workers) while holding constant another input (number of machines).

If we flip that idea over, we get some insights into the costs of production. If there are only three machines, then increasing how much output is produced becomes more and more costly. The additional cost (**marginal cost**) of producing additional output increases as the amount of output being produced rises. A factory produces spiral notebooks. Producing another 100 notebooks when production is currently 1,000 notebooks per day is less expensive than producing another 100 notebooks when production is currently 8,000 notebooks per day. Economists say: Once diminishing marginal returns set in, marginal costs rise.

Firms produce output because doing so generates **profit**. We assume that the goal of firms is to **maximize profit**. If an action increases profit, they will undertake the action. If an action decreases profit, they won't do it.

Profit is the difference between **revenue** and **costs**. So profit increases if revenue increases more than costs.

The notebook company is currently producing 6,000 notebooks per day. Should the company produce another 100 notebooks per day? The answer depends on the additional revenue (**marginal revenue**) from producing and selling the 100 notebooks and the additional cost (marginal cost) of producing the 100 notebooks. If the additional revenue exceeds the additional cost, the company should produce the 100 notebooks. Doing so would increase their profit.

But if the additional revenue from producing and selling the 100 notebooks is less than the additional cost, the company should not produce that 100 notebooks. Doing so would decrease their profit.

TRY

Answers to all "Try" questions are at the back of the book.

1. A firm receives $4,000 in revenue per week and incurs costs of $3,000 per week. What is its weekly profit?

2. Pepper's Pizza is currently producing 400 pizzas per week. Producing and selling an additional 40 pizzas per week would increase revenue by $400 and increase costs by $500. Will producing an additional 40 pizzas per week increase, decrease, or have no effect on Pepper's Pizza's profit?

PRODUCT CURVES, COST CURVES, AND PROFIT MAXIMIZATION

Now let's take this profit-maximization story, break it out, and add in the graphs. **Production** refers to combining inputs—labor, machines, materials, and so on—into output. Economists define the **short run** as a period of time when some inputs are fixed in quantity. Easy examples are the square footage of the business and the number of machines. **Capital** refers to buildings and machines. So economists often say: In the short run, the amount of capital is fixed.

The **long run** is defined as a period of time long enough that the quantities of all inputs can be changed. A business can sell its building or get out of its lease. Machinery can be sold or purchased.

The number of days or weeks or months in the short run and the long run is not preset. The length of time depends on the industry. Compare a taxi driver and a car manufacturer. The **fixed capital** for the taxi driver is the car and the taxi license. If the taxi driver decides to leave the industry, how many days does it take to get rid of the car and the license? Not many. Or if you decide to become a taxi driver, how many days does it take to lease a car and obtain the license? Again, not many. For a car manufacturer, the fixed capital is the plant and equipment. If the car manufacturer decides to leave the industry, how many days (or, years!) does it take to sell off the plant and equipment? Months and months and months. The long run is a longer period of time for a car manufacturer than it is for a taxi driver.

In the short run, the amount of capital is fixed. So changing the amount of output produced is a matter of changing the other inputs, the **variable inputs**. As more inputs are added to a fixed amount of capital, more output is produced. The additional output produced when one more input is used is called the **marginal product** of that input.

A business with three machines and four workers is currently producing 100 units of output per day. When a fifth worker is employed, **total product** rises from 100 to 110 units of output. The marginal product of the fifth worker is 10 units of output.

When a business first starts hiring workers, some specialization can take place. The total product of the firm rises quickly. But at some point, because the amount of capital is fixed, additional workers simply can't contribute as much output. Economists say: Marginal product initially rises and then, once diminishing returns set in, declines as the variable input rises.

The **production function** shows how total product depends on the variable input. The production function (or, total product) and marginal product curves are depicted in Figure 6.1.

TRY

3. The "long run" for Starbucks, a large international chain of coffee shops, is many weeks or months longer than the "long run" for an artist who sells paintings at weekend arts and crafts fairs. Why?

4. 10 workers with 2 ovens can together produce 400 pizzas per week. 11 workers with 2 ovens can together produce 430 pizzas per week. 12 workers with 2 ovens can together produce 455 pizzas per week. What is the marginal product of the 11th worker? Of the 12th worker?

Cost Curves

The production relationships determine the costs of production. In the short run (when capital is fixed), producing more output requires more of the variable input. When firms hire more workers, the **total cost** of production rises.

Total costs are divided into two categories. **Fixed costs** are the costs of the fixed input, which is usually capital. Remember, the fixed inputs are those that

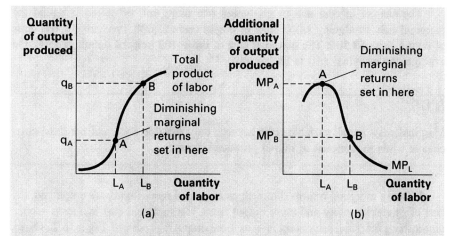

Figure 6.1 Total and marginal product curves.

The production function in Figure 6.1a shows the total quantity of output produced with varying quantities of the variable input, labor. When the quantity of labor is L_A, total output is q_A. When the quantity of labor is L_B, total output is q_B. Diminishing marginal returns to labor set in at point A, where the total product curve is steepest. The marginal product of labor is graphed in Figure 6.1b. When the quantity of labor is L_A, the additional output produced by the next worker is MP_A. When the quantity of labor is L_B, the additional output produced by the next worker is MP_B. Diminishing marginal returns set in at point A, where the marginal product curve reaches its maximum.

cannot be changed in the short run. Fixed costs do not depend on the amount of output produced. No output, lots of output, or something in between—the fixed costs are the same dollar amount.

The second category of costs are called **variable costs**. Variable costs are the costs of paying for the variable input. Variable costs vary (or, change) as the amount of output produced changes. No output, no variable costs. Lots of output, lots of variable costs.

TRY

5. In the following scenario, which costs are fixed costs and which are variable costs?

Sherry runs a hair salon. She rents the space for $4,000 a month. Her electricity bill is about $400 a month. She has purchased several shampoo sinks and styling stations for a total of $5,000. Her insurance costs $6,000 a year. Sherry has two employees who help with shampooing, scheduling, and other tasks and she pays each $11 an hour. She uses about $100 of shampoo and other hair products each week.

The change in cost due to producing one more unit of output is called the marginal cost. Producing 1,000 units of output costs $3,000. Producing 1,100 units of output costs $3,500. The marginal cost of those 100 units of output is $500. On average, the marginal cost is $5 per unit.

TIP

Marginal costs are all variable costs because only variable costs and not fixed costs change when the amount of output produced changes.

Because marginal returns diminish as more and more inputs are employed, the cost of producing more and more output rises. The marginal cost increases—once diminishing marginal returns set in—as more output is produced. Figure 6.2a shows a **marginal cost curve**.

Average total cost is total cost divided by quantity produced:

Average total cost = total cost / quantity of output produced

When the quantity produced is low, average total costs (ATC) fall as quantity produced rises. The fixed costs are spread over more and more units of output, lowering ATC. But eventually as quantity produced rises, average total costs rise, too. Rising **average variable costs** due to diminishing marginal returns overwhelm falling **average fixed costs**, raising ATC. See Figure 6.2b.

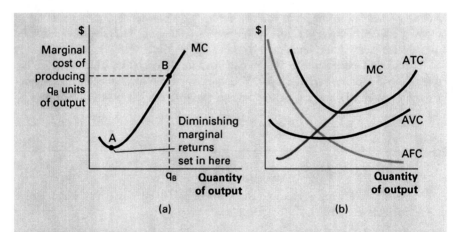

Figure 6.2 Cost curves.

Once diminishing marginal returns set in at point A in Figure 6.2a, marginal costs (MC) rise as more output is produced. Average cost curves are shown in Figure 6.2b. Average fixed cost (AFC) falls over the entire range of output. Average total cost (ATC) and average variable cost (AVC) both fall at initially low levels of output, then hit a minimum, then rise as output increases further.

TIP

The average total cost (ATC) curve falls until it crosses the marginal cost (MC) curve. Then after it crosses MC, ATC rises. So ATC hits its minimum just as it crosses MC.

TRY

6. Draw a graph that shows typical MC and ATC curves. What can you say about the point where the MC and ATC curves intersect or cross?

7. When 100 dolls are manufactured per day, total costs are $200. When 101 dolls are manufactured per day, total costs are $212.10. What is the average total cost when output is 100 dolls per day? What is the average total cost when output is 101 dolls per day? What is the marginal cost of manufacturing the 101st doll?

8. In the short run, when the number of dolls manufactured increases from 100 to 101 dolls per day, which type of costs increases—fixed costs or variable costs?

LONG-RUN AVERAGE COST

The short run is a period of time short enough that the amount of capital—machinery and buildings—is fixed. The long run is a period of time long enough that the firm can change the amount of capital. A firm will adjust the amount of its capital as the amount of output they are producing—the **scale of production**—changes.

A firm producing a small amount of output will have a small number of machines. How many ovens are in a neighborhood bakery? A firm producing a lot of output will have a lot of machines. How many ovens are in the Wonder Bread bakery? The scale of production is much greater in the Wonder Bread bakery than it is in the neighborhood bakery.

Once a firm has decided how many machines it needs—the neighborhood bakery has installed two ovens—then it is operating in the short run. Its marginal cost will rise as it produces more output, due to diminishing marginal returns to the variable inputs. The average total cost (ATC) curve will have its usual shape. At low levels of output, the firm's average total costs will initially fall, then hit a minimum when average total costs equal marginal cost, and then rise as output continues to increase.

But if the firm increases how much it is producing, it is likely to adjust the amount of capital. The neighborhood bakery has become very popular. In order to get all its baked goods ready before the morning rush, the cooks are starting their baking at 1:00 A.M. The bakery owners decide to buy another oven so the staff can come to work at a more decent hour. Buying an oven is changing the amount of capital, so this is a long-run decision.

Once the third machine is installed, the firm's costs of production change. Buying the third oven lowers the bakery's average costs of meeting the current level of demand. Again, as its output rises, the firm's average total costs will initially fall, then hit a minimum when average total costs equal marginal cost, and then rise as output continues to increase.

Figure 6.3a captures the story thus far. MC_2 and ATC_2 are the cost curves when the bakery has two ovens. At a high level of output, the firm decides to purchase a third oven. The third oven lowers the average total cost of producing that level of output, and shifts the marginal cost to MC_3.

Imagine now all the possible levels of output for the neighborhood bakery. With enough time and planning, the bakery will adjust the number of machines according to how much it is producing. A graph that shows the average cost of producing each possible level of output, allowing the firm to change not just the variable inputs but also the fixed input of capital, is called the **long-run average total cost curve**. See Figure 6.3b.

Depending on the characteristics of the firm and of its production, long-run average total cost could rise, fall, or stay the same as the amount being produced increases. When long-run average total cost is constant as a firm's scale—the amount being produced—increases, economists say the firm is exhibiting **constant returns to scale**. The long-run average total cost curve will be a horizontal line.

When the long-run average total cost falls as its scale rises, economists say the firm is exhibiting **economies of scale**, or **increasing returns to scale**. The long-run average total cost curve will slope downward.

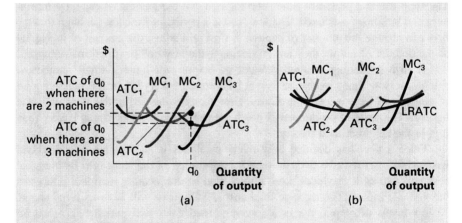

Figure 6.3 Long-run cost curves.

In the long run, firms change the amount of capital as output changes. In Figure 6.3a, the average total cost of producing q_0 units of output is higher when the firm owns just two machines (ATC_2) than when it owns three machines (ATC_3). The long-run average total cost (LRATC) curve in Figure 6.3b shows the average total costs of producing each level of output in the long run, when the firm is free to change the amount of capital it uses.

When the long-run average total cost rises as its scale rises, economists say the firm is exhibiting **diseconomies of scale**, or **decreasing returns to scale**. The long-run average total cost curve will slope upward.

MAXIMIZING PROFIT

Profit is the difference between revenue and costs. Many textbooks express this relationship with an equation:

$$Profit = Total\ revenue\ (TR) - Total\ costs\ (TC)$$

Revenue is the money the firm receives from selling its output. Revenue is equal to price times quantity.

To maximize profit, firms should produce the quantity of output where marginal revenue equals marginal cost. This is the **profit-maximizing condition**.

To maximize profit, produce the quantity where $MR = MC$

TYPES OF INDUSTRIES

How a firm maximizes profit depends on the type of industry it is in. Economists identify four types of industries based on the type of competition that takes place in the industry: perfect competition, monopoly, monopolistic competition, and oligopoly.

Perfect Competition. A perfectly competitive industry is characterized as

- an industry with many small firms,
- none of which has a large share of the total market,
- producing a homogeneous product,
- in an industry in which there are no barriers to entry into or exit from the industry.

Monopoly. There is just one firm in a monopolized industry. Other firms cannot enter the industry. So the characteristics of monopoly are

- an industry with just one firm,
- producing a unique product,
- in an industry in which there are barriers to entry.

Monopolistic Competition. This is a blend of monopoly and perfect competition. The characteristics of monopolistic competition are

- an industry with many firms,
- producing a product for which the competitors sell close but not perfect substitutes,
- in an industry in which there are no barriers to entry into or exit from the industry.

Oligopoly. An industry that is an oligopoly is characterized as

- an industry with perhaps many or perhaps few firms,
- a handful (three or four) of firms that together hold a very large (80–90 percent) market share,
- producing a product that may or may not be homogeneous,
- in an industry in which there may or may not be barriers to entry.

TRY

9. For each of the following products, is the industry characterized by perfect competition, monopoly, monopolistic competition, or oligopoly?
   - Zucchini squash sold at the local farmers' market
   - Airline flights
   - Restaurant meals

The upward-sloping supply curve of the supply and demand model is for *perfectly competitive* firms only. The other three types of industries—monopoly, monopolistic competition, and oligopoly—are all considered forms of **imperfect competition**. In this chapter, we look at how perfectly competitive firms maximize profit. How other firms maximize profit is considered in Chapter 7.

TIP

So far, nothing in our story depends on the type of industry. Everything up to (but not beyond) this point applies in perfect competition, monopoly, monopolistic competition, or oligopoly.

For the perfectly competitive firm, prices are determined by market supply and market demand. The firm takes the price as given. Economists say: Perfectly competitive firms are **price takers**.

The firm charges every customer the same price. So if the firm sells one more unit of output, its additional **revenue** is the price of that unit of output. Economists say: For the perfectly competitive firm, **marginal revenue** equals the price.

Economists often show this relationship with a graph. The marginal revenue curve is a horizontal line because marginal revenue for the perfectly competitive firm simply equals the price. The marginal cost curve is upward sloping. The profit-maximizing quantity is found where the marginal revenue curve and marginal cost curve intersect. See Figure 6.4a.

If the market price rises, the perfectly competitive firm's profit-maximizing quantity rises also, as shown in Figure 6.4b. For the firm, the marginal cost curve traces out the firm's individual supply curve. Add up all the individual supply curves for all the firms in the industry and you have the market supply curve.

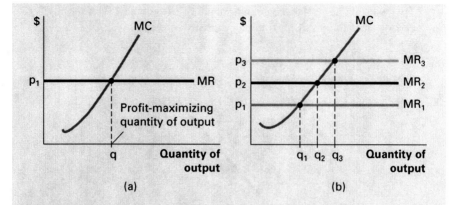

Figure 6.4 Marginal cost and marginal revenue.

The profit-maximizing firm produces a quantity of output where marginal revenue (MR) equals marginal cost (MC). The perfectly competitive firm faces a horizontal marginal revenue curve, as shown in Figure 6.4a. As the market price rises, the quantity supplied by the firm rises as well, as shown in Figure 6.4b.

So why does supply slope up? Ultimately, because the marginal cost curve slopes up. Why does the marginal cost curve slope up? Because of the law of diminishing marginal returns.

TRY

10. Label the axes and curves in the graph below. Show the profit-maximizing quantity of output.

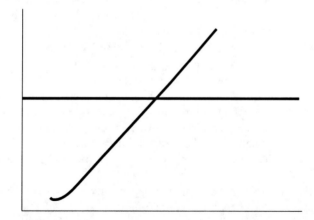

11. Use the graph below to answer these questions. When the price is p_1, what is the profit-maximizing quantity of output? When the price is

p_2, what is the profit-maximizing quantity of output? When the price is p_3, what is the profit-maximizing quantity of output?

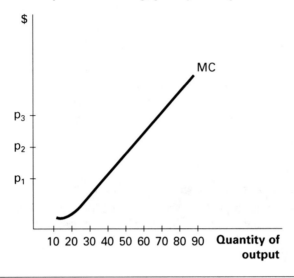

PROFIT

Economists distinguish between two measures of profit: **accounting profit** and **economic profit**. Accounting profit is the figure a business would report on its taxes or in its annual reports. It is the difference between revenues and operating costs.

A local bakery has an accounting profit of $50,000 a year. Is that good or bad? Without some measure of comparison, you can't answer the question. If the owner has given up the opportunity to earn $80,000 a year working for someone else, then $50,000 is not so good. The owner could earn $30,000 more a year by closing the business and working for someone else.

But if the best the owner could do by working for someone else is to earn $40,000 a year, then a $50,000 accounting profit is good. The owner is doing better running the bakery than he could working for someone else.

Economists formalize these comparisons by calculating *economic profit*. Economic profit equals accounting profit minus the business owner's opportunity cost of running the business. Has the business owner taken some money out of savings and used it to buy capital? Then the foregone interest earnings on the savings is part of his opportunity cost. Economists call this the **normal rate of return on capital**.

Has the business owner passed up the opportunity to work for someone else? Then the foregone salary is part of his opportunity cost.

An economic profit of zero is good. It means the owner is doing as well in this business as he could doing anything else. An economic profit greater than zero is amazingly good. It means the owner is doing better in this business than he could doing anything else. An economic profit below zero (a loss) is bad. It means the owner is doing worse in this business than he could doing something else.

How Much Profit

The firm's total profit equals its total revenue minus total costs. Total revenue is price times quantity. Total cost is average total cost times quantity. So total profit is

$$\textit{Total profit} = (\textit{price} - \textit{average total cost}) \times \textit{quantity}$$

Total profit is equal to the area of the rectangle whose base is the profit-maximizing quantity and whose height is the difference between the price and the average total cost at that quantity.

If price is greater than average total cost as in Figure 6.5a, profit is positive. Economists say: The firm is earning an **abnormal profit**.

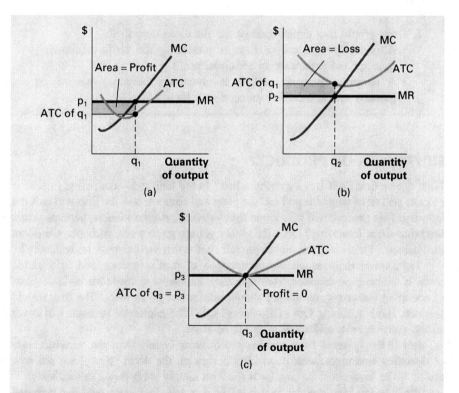

Figure 6.5 How much profit?

In Figure 6.5a, the price is above the average total cost at the profit-maximizing quantity, and so the firm earns an abnormal profit. In Figure 6.5b, the price is below the average total cost at the profit-maximizing quantity, and so the firm incurs a loss. In Figure 6.5c, the price equals the average total cost at the profit-maximizing quantity, and so the firm's profit is zero, a normal profit.

If price is less than average total cost as in Figure 6.5b, profit is negative. Economists say: The firm is earning an **economic loss**.

If price just equals average total cost as in Figure 6.5c, profit is zero. Economists say: The firm is earning **normal profit**.

Why would a firm stay in business if its profit was zero? Remember that the profit we are measuring here is *economic profit*. One of the costs is opportunity cost—what would the business owner earn in her next best alternative? When economic profit equals zero, accounting profit equals what the owner could earn elsewhere. When a business owner has zero economic profit, she is doing as well in that business as she could anywhere else. If she could earn $60,000 annually doing something else, then an economic profit of zero is the same as an accounting profit of $60,000 a year.

TRY

12. Draw graphs that depict each of the situations described.
    - A perfectly competitive firm is producing the profit-maximizing quantity and is earning an abnormal profit.
    - A perfectly competitive firm is producing the profit-maximizing quantity and is incurring an economic loss.

SHUT DOWN OR PRODUCE?

What does a firm do if it is incurring a loss? In the long run—the period of time it takes to get out of contracts and sell the plant and equipment—the firm will **exit** the industry. This process will take some time—weeks, maybe months, perhaps years. But what about tomorrow? Does the owner get up, go to work, and open the doors for business? Or should the owner instead shut down the business immediately?

The answer depends on the comparison of firm's revenue and its variable costs. If the revenue received from operating tomorrow exceeds the variable costs of operating tomorrow, the owner should get up and go to work. The firm should produce. Have a "Going Out of Business" sale. The additional revenue will cover all the variable costs and some of the fixed costs.

But if the revenue from operating tomorrow is less than the variable costs of operating tomorrow, shut down. Put a sign on the door: "Sorry, we are now closed." The losses will be smaller if the firm simply shuts down immediately.

What is intuitive can be expressed in a graph. In Figure 6.6, the marginal revenue and marginal cost curves determine the profit-maximizing quantity. The average total cost curve and the price determine the economic loss. The short-run decision of shut down or produce comes from a comparison of the average variable cost curve and the price. If the price falls below the average variable cost, the firm should immediately shut down to minimize losses. Economists call the minimum of the average variable cost curve the **shut-down point**.

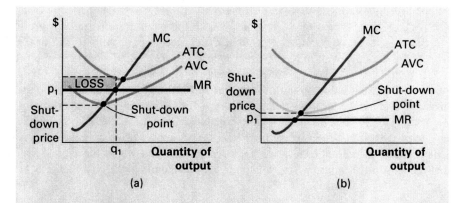

Figure 6.6 Shut-down point.

A firm that is incurring a loss will exit the industry in the long run. In the short run, whether the firm continues to produce or immediately shuts down depends on a comparison of the price and the average variable cost. In Figure 6.6a the firm will continue to produce in the short run because the price of its output is greater than the average variable cost of producing q_1 units of output. The firm's losses are smaller in the short run by producing. In Figure 6.6b, the firm will shut down immediately because the price of its output is less than the minimum average variable cost. The firm's losses are smaller in the short run if it does not produce and simply pays its fixed costs.

TRY

13. A profit-maximizing firm is producing and selling 100 units of output per day. It sells its output at a market price of $6 per unit. When the firm is producing 100 units of output, the firm's ATC is $6.50 and its AVC is $4.80. Is the firm earning a profit or a loss? What is the dollar amount of this profit or loss? In the long run, should the firm continue in this industry, or exit the industry? In the short run, should the firm continue to produce, or shut down?

14. A profit-maximizing firm is producing and selling 40 units of output per day. It sells its output at a market price of $75 per unit. When the firm is producing 40 units of output, the firm's ATC is $90 and its AVC is $82. Is the firm earning a profit or a loss? What is the dollar amount of this profit or loss? In the long run, should the firm continue in this industry, or exit the industry? In the short run, should the firm continue to produce, or shut down?

IN THE LONG RUN, ECONOMIC PROFIT EQUALS ZERO

An important feature of perfectly competitive firms is the absence of barriers to entry into or exit from the industry. The free flow of firms into and out of a perfectly competitive industry means that in the long run, the typical firm in a perfectly competitive industry will earn zero economic profit. Firms earning zero economic profit are earning a positive accounting profit. Zero economic profit tells us the firm's owners are doing as well in their current industry as they could anywhere else.

If a firm in a perfectly competitive industry is incurring losses, in the long run it will exit the industry: the owners will sell off the equipment and close the business. The number of firms in the industry will fall, lowering the market supply. As market supply falls, price rises. Firms that have remained in the industry will be able to raise their prices, lowering their losses. The number of firms in the industry will continue to fall until the price has risen to the point where the typical firm that remains in the industry is now earning zero economic profit. See Figure 6.7a.

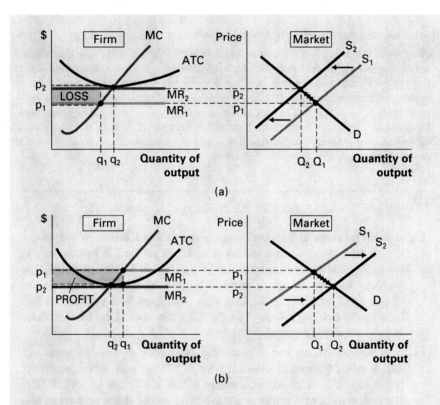

Figure 6.7 In the long run, economic profit equals zero.

When firms in perfectly competitive industries incur losses as in Figure 6.7a, firms exit the industry. The resulting decrease in market supply raises market price from p_1 to p_2. Losses of firms that remain in the industry are reduced. Firms will exit the industry until the price rises to p_2 where profit of the remaining firms equals zero.

When firms earn abnormal profit as in Figure 6.7b, new firms will enter the industry. The increased market supply lowers the price, eroding the profit of existing firms. Supply will continue to increase and prices will continue to fall until the price falls to p_2, where profit of all firms equals zero.

If firms in a perfectly competitive industry are earning abnormal profit, other firms will enter the industry: other people will open competing firms in the same industry. The number of firms in the industry will rise, increasing the market supply. As market supply rises, price falls. As firms in the industry lower their prices due to competition, profits decline. The number of firms in the industry will continue to rise until the price has fallen to the point where the typical firm in the industry is earning zero economic profit. See Figure 6.7b.

A perfectly competitive firm produces a profit-maximizing quantity where price equals marginal cost. In the long run, the perfectly competitive firm will produce a profit-maximizing quantity where price also equals the minimum of the average total cost curve. In the long run, a perfectly competitive firm will earn zero economic profit.

TRY

15. Can perfectly competitive firms continue to earn abnormal profit in the long run? Why or why not?

Chapter 7

Imperfect Competition

Businesses maximize profit by producing the quantity of output at which marginal revenue equals marginal cost. That is the *universal* profit-maximization rule. How that rule plays out depends on the type of industry. When a business is maximizing profit in perfectly competitive industries, price equals marginal cost. But what about when there is imperfect competition? In this chapter, we examine profit-maximizing behavior by firms in each of the industries characterized by imperfect competition: monopoly, monopolistic competition, and oligopoly.

KEY TERMS AND CONCEPTS

- Barriers to entry
- Government franchises
- Patents
- Natural monopoly
- Price takers
- Price maker
- Marginal revenue
- Quantity effect
- Price effect
- Monopolistic competition
- Oligopoly
- Cartel
- Collusion
- Antitrust laws
- Cournot model
- Duopoly
- Price-leadership model
- Predatory pricing
- Kinked demand curve model
- Game theory
- Strategic behavior
- Payoff
- Prisoners' dilemma
- Payoff matrix

- Dominant strategy
- Nash equilibrium

KEY EQUATION

- Profit-maximization rule

KEY GRAPHS

- Profit-maximization for a monopoly
- Long-run equilibrium in monopolistic competition
- Kinked demand curve

MONOPOLY

A monopoly is an industry with one firm. **Barriers to entry** prevent other firms from entering the industry. Sources of barriers to entry vary.

- Local government may license just one company to operate in a town. A common example is cable television companies. Economists say: **Government franchises** can provide a firm with a monopoly.
- Knowledge of a necessary invention or production process may be restricted to one company. To protect rights to intellectual property, governments issue **patents**, legal exclusive rights to an invention or a process.
- Due to high fixed costs, profitability may be possible only with a very high scale of production. Economists call this a **natural monopoly**.
- A scarce natural resource that is necessary to production may be owned by just one company, providing it with a monopoly.

When a firm is a monopoly, it faces the entire market demand. The contrast with perfect competition is stark. When a firm is part of a perfectly competitive industry, it faces such a tiny part of the entire market demand that whether the firm produces nothing or produces all it possibly can, its behavior has no influence on the market price. Put another way: When just one firm leaves a perfectly competitive industry, the reduction in market quantity supplied is so small that it is almost impossible to see the difference between the initial and the new market supply curves. Firms in a perfectly competitive industry are thus called **price takers** because they take the price as "given."

A monopoly firm is instead a **price maker**. It is the only firm supplying output to the market. Its behavior determines the market price. If the firm wants to bring in more customers, it must lower the price of its product. If the firm raises its price, it will lose customers. The monopoly firm decides what the price will be.

Marginal revenue is the change in revenue from selling one more unit of output. For the perfectly competitive firm, the marginal revenue is just the price of output. The perfectly competitive firm cannot change the market price. So if it sells one more unit of output, the perfectly competitive firm will sell that output at the market price. Its marginal revenue equals the market price.

For the monopolist, marginal revenue is not the market price. When a monopoly sells more output, two opposing forces are at work. Selling more output increases revenue, so this **quantity effect** increases revenue. But because demand curves slope down, selling more output requires lowering the price, so this **price effect** decreases revenue. Sometimes the quantity effect dominates the price effect: An increase in output has the overall effect of increasing revenue, so marginal revenue is positive. Other times the price effect dominates the quantity effect: An increase in output lowers revenue, so marginal revenue is negative.

TIP

Elasticity shows up here. When lowering the price raises total revenue, marginal revenue is positive and demand is price elastic. When lowering the price decreases total revenue, marginal revenue is negative and demand is price inelastic.

By and large, the quantity effect dominates at relatively low levels of output. The price effect dominates at relatively high levels of output. Demand and marginal revenue for the monopolist appear in Figure 7.1. When output is below q*, marginal revenue is positive. When output is above q*, marginal revenue is negative. At low levels of output, marginal revenue is positive and demand is price elastic. At high levels of output, marginal revenue is negative and demand is price inelastic.

TIP

When you draw a marginal revenue curve, it should split the distance between the vertical axis and the demand curve.

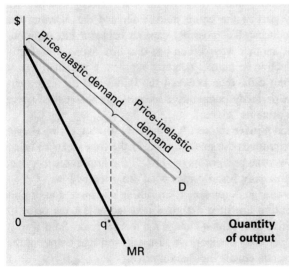

Figure 7.1 Demand and marginal revenue for a monopolist.

The monopolist faces the entire downward-sloping demand curve. Its marginal revenue curve is also downward sloping. When the quantity of output is less than q*, marginal revenue is positive and demand is price elastic. When the quantity of output is greater than q*, marginal revenue is negative and demand is price inelastic.

TRY

Answers to all "Try" questions are at the book of the book.

1. Draw the marginal revenue curve for the monopolist's demand curve depicted below.

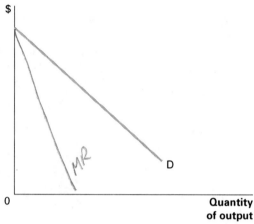

2. When price falls from $30 to $28, demand for the monopolist's output increases from 100 to 101 units. How big is the quantity effect? How big is the price effect? What is the marginal revenue when quantity increases from 100 to 101?

Marginal cost is not affected by the type of firm. Monopolists, like perfectly competitive firms, face an upward-sloping marginal cost curve due to diminishing marginal returns. Average costs also are unaffected by the type of the firm. Monopolists face an average total cost curve that falls until it crosses the marginal cost curve and then subsequently rises.

Any firm of any type maximizes profit by producing the quantity at which marginal revenue equals marginal cost. This is the universal profit-maximization rule:

To maximize profit, produce the quantity where MR = MC

The monopolist's situation is illustrated in Figure 7.2. To maximize profit, the monopolist produces a level of output q_M at which marginal revenue equals marginal cost.

What price does the monopolist charge? The monopolist charges the maximum possible price that allows it to sell all the output it produces. The monopolist relies on its demand curve, not its marginal revenue curve, to determine the price of its output. The demand curve tells us that p_M is the maximum price buyers will pay for q_M units of output. If the monopolist sets the price above p_M, quantity demanded will fall below q_M, leaving unsold output in inventory. If the monopolist sets the price below p_M, quantity demanded will rise above q_M and some customers will walk away frustrated by their inability to buy the product.

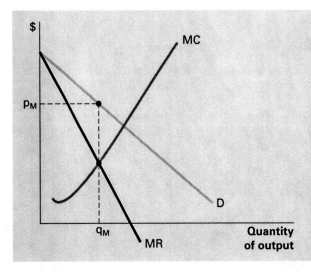

Figure 7.2 Profit maximization for a monopolist.

The profit-maximizing monopolist will produce the quantity q_M where marginal revenue equals marginal cost. It will charge p_M, the maximum price it can charge and still sell q_M units of output.

TIP

Because marginal cost is always positive, marginal revenue will always be positive when it equals marginal cost, so the monopolist will always produce in the price-elastic range of the demand curve.

TRY

3. A monopolist faces the demand curve and marginal cost curve shown at the right. Show on the graph the monopolist's profit-maximizing quantity and the price it should charge.

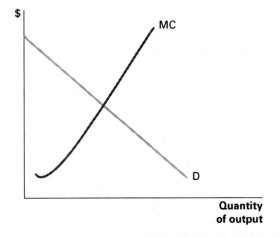

How much profit is the monopolist earning? Profit is the difference between total revenue and total cost.

$$Profit = Total\ revenue - Total\ cost$$

Total revenue equals price times quantity. Price is given by the demand curve and quantity is the profit-maximizing quantity. Total cost equals average total cost times quantity. So to determine how much profit the monopolist earns requires one more piece of information: average total cost. Calculation of profit is shown in Figure 7.3.

The monopolist typically earns abnormal profit. Its price is typically above its average total cost. Why don't others enter the industry and compete away the monopolist's profit? Because barriers to entry prevent competitors from entering the industry. Monopolists face no long-run erosion of profit through competition.

TRY

4. When a monopolist produces and sells 500 units of output per day, its marginal cost and marginal revenue both equal $47. The average total cost of producing 500 units of output is $60 per unit. The monopolist can sell all 500 units of output each day when the price is $65 per unit. Sketch a graph of a profit-maximizing monopolist. Use the info in this question to label your graph.

5. In question 4, how much profit is the monopolist earning?

6. Can the monopolist continue to earn abnormal profit in the long run? Why?

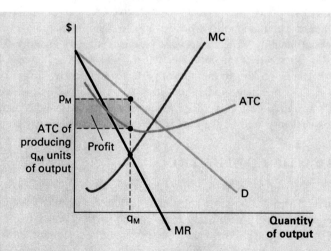

Figure 7.3 How much profit?

Profit is the area of the rectangle whose base is the quantity sold, q_M, and whose height is the difference between the price, p_M, and the average total cost of producing q_M units of output.

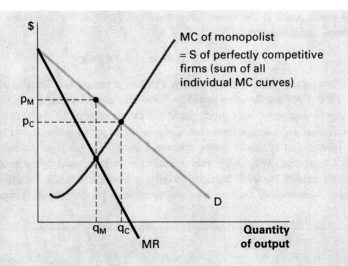

Figure 7.4 Comparing monopoly and perfect competition.

The monopolist charges price, p_M, and sells a profit-maximizing quantity, q_M. If the industry were instead perfectly competitive, price, p_C, would be below the monopolist's price and quantity, q_C, would be above the monopolist's quantity.

Can the monopolist charge any price? No. The monopolist is constrained by the demand curve. If the monopolist's price is too high, quantity demanded will fall off.

Does the monopolist charge the same price as a perfectly competitive firm? No. The absence of competition keeps prices high. The monopolist's price is greater than a competitive price. The perfectly competitive firm charges a price equal to its marginal cost. The monopolist's price is greater than its marginal cost.

What about quantity? The monopolist produces a lower quantity than would be produced in a perfectly competitive market. We show this in Figure 7.4. Pretend the monopoly can be broken up into lots of perfectly competitive firms. The market supply curve, the sum of the individual firms' supply curves, is the same as the monopolist's marginal cost curve. The monopolist's price is higher and quantity produced lower than would be the case if the market were perfectly competitive.

MONOPOLISTIC COMPETITION

Monopoly is an industry with one firm that faces the entire downward-sloping demand curve. There are no close substitutes for the monopolist's output. Perfect competition is an industry with many firms and no barriers preventing other firms from entering the industry. Each firm's output cannot be distinguished from every other firm's output. So each firm's output is a perfect substitute for any other firm's output. **Monopolistic competition** is a blend of monopoly and perfect competition.

Like perfect competition, an industry characterized by monopolistic competition has many firms, and no barriers to entry. But in contrast to perfect competition, each firm in a monopolistically competitive industry is producing a distinguishable

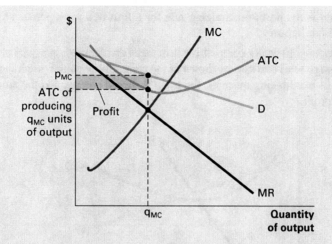

Figure 7.5 Monopolistic competition.

A firm in a monopolistically competitive industry faces a downward-sloping demand curve that is relatively price elastic. The profit-maximizing firm produces the quantity, q_{MC}, where marginal revenue equals marginal cost. It charges the price, p_{MC}. The firm's profit is equal to the area of the rectangle whose base is the quantity sold, q_{MC}, and whose height is the difference between the price, p_{MC}, and the average total cost of producing q_{MC} units of output.

product. The competing firms offer products that are close but not perfect substitutes. So each firm faces a downward-sloping demand curve. But because there are close substitutes, the demand for any firm's product is relatively elastic.

On a day-to-day basis, we each interact with monopolistically competitive firms. University towns have many coffee houses, each of which distinguishes its product slightly from its competitors. Hair salons and restaurants are also monopolistically competitive firms. Most small businesses in most towns fall into this category.

The universal profit-maximization rule applies universally.

To maximize profit, produce the quantity where MR = MC

The firm in a monopolistically competitive industry produces the quantity q_{MC} where marginal revenue equals marginal cost. It charges the maximum price possible, which is read off its demand curve. Its profit is equal to the area of the rectangle whose base is the quantity produced and whose height is the difference between price and average total cost. See Figure 7.5.

TRY

7. What are the differences between perfect competition and monopolistic competition? What are the differences between monopoly and monopolistic competition?

8. What is the profit-maximizing rule for a firm in a monopolistically competitive industry?

9. A monopolistically competitive firm faces the demand, marginal cost, and average total cost curves shown at the right. Show on the graph the firm's profit-maximizing quantity, the price it should charge, and the amount of its profit.

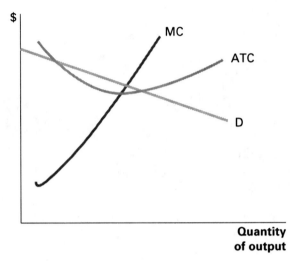

So far monopoly and monopolistic competition appear to be the same. The only difference so far is that the demand faced by a firm in a monopolistically competitive industry will always be relatively elastic over the entire reasonable range of output.

No barriers to entry is the most important difference between monopoly and monopolistic competition. Because there are no barriers to entry in monopolistic competititon, new firms will enter an industry whose firms are earning abnormal profit. Competition erodes profit in the long run.

Wanda's Donut Shop is one of several donut shops in town. Wanda offers free newspapers and clean restrooms, distinguishing her shop from many others. Business has been good and Wanda is earning more running the donut shop than she could doing anything else. Her economic profit is greater than zero. She is earning abnormal profit.

Word gets around town that there is money to be made in donuts. Warren opens a new donut shop down the street from Wanda's. Many of Wanda's customers are loyal to her, but not all. Some are intrigued by the comfortable chairs and convenient parking available at Warren's. Demand for Wanda's donuts decreases as some customers substitute Warren's donuts for hers.

As demand for Wanda's donuts decreases, she cuts her prices slightly and produces fewer donuts. If Wanda and Warren and other donut shops continue to earn abnormal profits, more competitors will open donut shops. New shops will

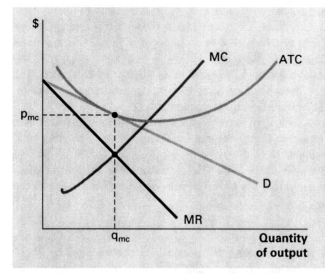

Figure 7.6 Monopolistic competition in long-run equilibrium.

In the long run, the firm in a monopolistically competitive industry will earn zero economic profit. Competition will reduce demand for its product, shifting its demand curve to the left, until price, p_{MC}, equals average total cost at the profit-maximizing quantity of output q_{MC}.

open until the money to be made in donuts is no greater than what can be made in other lines of business. Economists say: Businesses will enter the industry until competition reduces profit to zero.

In the long run, each firm in a monopolistically competitive industry will earn zero profit. This long-run equilibrium is shown in Figure 7.6. In the long run, a firm in a monopolistically competitive industry charges a price above its marginal cost but equal to its average total cost.

TRY

10. In the long run, how much profit does a typical firm in a monopolistically competitive industry earn? Why?

11. Why would anyone own a business if their maximum economic profit was just zero?

12. Wanda was initially earning abnormal economic profit. Which curve(s) in Figure 7.5 should you shift to get to Figure 7.6's depiction of zero economic profit?

OLIGOPOLY

Oligopoly is the third and final category of imperfect competition. Every industry that is not a monopoly, perfectly competitive, or monopolistically competitive is an oligopoly. It is hard to say anything definitive about oligopolies because there is so much variation within the category.

How many firms are there in an oligopoly? Sometimes just a few. Sometimes a lot. There is no strict rule. What is almost always true of an oligopoly is that a handful of firms dominate the industry, producing the vast majority of total output. An industry with four firms is an oligopoly. An industry with 1,000 firms, just four of which control 80 percent of the market, is an oligopoly. The key: a few firms dominate the industry.

What can we say about the output produced in an oligopoly? Not much. The firms may produce a homogeneous output. They may produce differentiated output. There is no strict rule. The key: a few firms dominate the industry.

What about barriers to entry? Can we say something definitive there? No. There may be barriers to entry. There may not be. Again, there is no strict rule. The key: a few firms dominate the industry.

How do the businesses maximize profit? Here we can make a definitive statement. The profit-maximization rule is a universal rule, and does not depend on the type of industry.

To maximize profit, produce the quantity where MR = MC

Because there is so much variation among industries characterized by oligopoly, there are many different models to explain how firms behave. Each model makes a different assumption about how the firms relate to each other. Here is a taste of the variety of models.

TRY

13. What is the only definitive statement we can make about oligopoly?

Collusion Model

When there are just a handful of firms in an industry, they might get together and collectively decide how much to produce and what price to charge. Economists say: The firms are a **cartel**. The most famous cartel is OPEC, the Organization of Petroleum Exporting Countries. In the United States, such **collusion** is illegal because it violates our federal **antitrust laws**.

When firms form a cartel, they behave like a monopoly. The profit-maximizing quantity is the quantity where marginal revenue equals marginal cost. The price charged will be greater than the marginal cost.

Cournot Model

When there are just two profit-maximizing firms in an industry, and each firm decides how much to produce after taking into account how much the other firm is producing, the **Cournot model** describes how much each firm will produce. Economists call an industry with just two firms a **duopoly**.

This model is essentially monopolistic competition with just two firms. Competition between the two firms continually shifts each firm's demand curve to the left. Ultimately the firms both settle at an equilibrium at which they are splitting the market and charging the same price. Because there are just two firms, abnormal profit is likely.

Most economists think this model is naive. It assumes that each firm reacts to but does not anticipate the other's behavior. Yet despite the model's naiveté, the conclusion makes some sense. If there are two ice cream vendors on a beach, they will probably wind up each selling about the same number of ice cream cones and charging the same price.

Price Leadership Model

When there is one dominant firm (think: Wal-Mart) and many smaller firms (think: local businesses also selling some of the same items), the dominant firm is likely to set the price. The smaller firms are forced to match the dominant firm's price or lose their customers. Economists call this a **price-leadership model**.

The dominant firm behaves like a monopolist, setting the profit-maximizing quantity where marginal revenue equals marginal cost and charging the price off of its demand curve. The smaller firms behave like perfectly competitive firms, taking the price set by the dominant firm as given.

What if the dominant firm's price is so low that the smaller firms incur losses and, in the long run, exit the industry? Ultimately the dominant firm will wind up with the entire market demand, increasing its profit. High long-run profit creates an incentive for the dominant firm to set the price very low, incur short-run losses, and wait out its competitors. Economists call this behavior **predatory pricing**. It is illegal in the United States. The dominant firm can set the price low if its costs are low. But it cannot legally set its price below costs as a strategy for eliminating competition.

Kinked Demand Curve Model

When there are a handful of firms in an industry, and each firm assumes that the other firms will follow a price cut but not a price increase, the **kinked demand curve model** describes firm behavior. The profit-maximizing quantity and price will not change even if the firm's costs of production change.

OfficeWay is one of three firms selling computer printers. All three firms are currently charging $119.99 for a particular printer. OfficeWay assumes that if it cuts its price of this printer, the other two firms will also cut their prices. So cutting prices does not allow OfficeWay to capture a greater share of the market. They will sell more printers—after all, demand curves slope down—but won't take business away from the competition.

What if OfficeWay raises its price above $119.99? OfficeWay assumes the other two firms will keep their prices unchanged. OfficeWay will lose market share as all but its most loyal customers flock to one of the other two stores. The demand for OfficeWay's printers is very elastic above the current price.

The resulting "kink" in the demand curve at the current price and quantity means the marginal revenue curve has a big gap in it at the current quantity. See Figure 7.7. The gap occurs at the current quantity and not the current price because

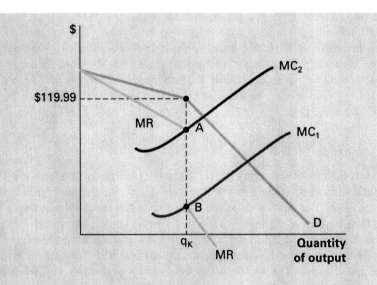

Figure 7.7 Kinked demand curve.

When OfficeWay assumes that all other firms will follow a price cut but not a price increase, the firm faces a demand curve that is kinked at the current price of $119.99. The kink creates a gap in the marginal revenue curve at the current quantity, q_K. The marginal cost of producing quantity q_K can be as high as A or as low as B and the profit-maximizing quantity will remain q_K and the price will remain $119.99.

marginal revenue is the change in revenue from a one-unit change in *quantity*. Each marginal revenue curve corresponds to the demand curve *at that quantity*.

So long as marginal cost is within the marginal revenue gap, the profit-maximizing quantity and price will be the same. In Figure 7.7, whether the marginal cost is as low as MC_1 or as high as MC_2 or anywhere in between, the firm maximizes profit by producing q_K units of output and charging $119.99 for each. Printers will be sold for $119.99 even if OfficeWay's costs rise as high as MC_1 or fall as low as MC_2.

Game Theory

When there are just a handful of firms, and each firm's behavior depends not just on what their competitors *have done* but also on what their competitors *might conceivably do*, **game theory** can describe behavior. Economists say: Game theory models **strategic behavior**.

A typical "game" includes two players and two strategies. For each player, the **payoff** to each strategy depends on what the other player does. A classic example is the **prisoners' dilemma**. This game is played out in many *Law and Order* episodes on cable TV. Harry and Johnny have been arrested for committing a crime together. If neither man testifies against the other, each will be sentenced to just 1 year in jail. The district attorney wants each man to testify against the other. A carefully designed set of offers is needed.

One assistant district attorney takes Harry into one room. The other assistant district attorney takes Johnny into the other room. If Harry promises to testify against Johnny and Johnny keeps quiet, Harry will get no jail time. But if Harry refuses to testify against Johnny, and Johnny testifies against Harry, then Harry will get a long jail sentence. Johnny receives the same offer.

What should each man do? If they could collude, both would agree to keep quiet. But Harry doesn't know if the assistant district attorney is being truthful when she says, "What are you going to do, Harry? Your buddy Johnny is in the other room singing like a lark. You keep quiet, Harry, and you're looking at 7 years in the slammer. You sing like Johnny, and we'll make it 3 years. So what's it going to be, Harry?"

Harry has to be strategic. His options are presented in Figure 7.8 in a table that economists call a **payoff matrix**. If Johnny has kept quiet, the best thing for Harry is to testify against Johnny. Harry will go free rather than spend 1 year in jail. If Johnny has promised to testify against Harry, the best thing for Harry is to testify against Johnny. Harry will get just 3 years rather than 7 years in jail. One strategy dominates: Whether Johnny keeps quiet or testifies against Harry, Harry's best strategy is to testify. Economists say: Harry has a **dominant strategy**.

	Harry testifies	Harry keeps quiet
Johnny testifies	Harry's sentence = 3 years	Harry's sentence = 7 years
Johnny keeps quiet	Harry's sentence = no jail time	Harry's sentence = 1 year

Figure 7.8 Harry's payoff matrix.

Harry's payoff matrix shows his jail time under each of two strategies: testifying or keeping quiet. Harry does not know what Johnny is going to do. If Johnny testifies (the top row), then Harry's best strategy is to testify: his jail time will be 3 years rather than 7 years. If Johnny keeps quiet (the bottom row), then Harry's best strategy is again to testify: he will have no jail time rather than 1 year. Testifying is Harry's dominant strategy because it is his best choice regardless of what Johnny does.

When everyone follows a strategy that gets them the best results, regardless of what their opponents are doing, economists say the result is a **Nash equilibrium**.

Determining a strategy that takes into account the range of possible actions of competitors is not just about two criminals in a scene out of *Law and Order*. Political scientists use game theory to analyze nuclear deterrence. Economists use game theory to analyze oligopoly behavior. It is a powerful tool currently permeating many fields in social science.

TRY

14. In each case below, which oligopoly model best describes behavior: collusion, Cournot, kinked demand, price leadership, or game theory?
    - There are only two fence-building companies in an isolated town. Each company has been in business for years. Although they started out charging different prices, each now charges the same price. Each company has about the same number of jobs per year.
    - In a town with six independent bookstores and one large chain bookstore, the independent bookstores struggle to match the low prices offered by the chain bookstore.
    - Four companies sell a similar product. Each believes that their price cuts will be matched by the competitors. Each also believes their price increases will not be followed by the others.
    - A business is deciding when to introduce a new model of their product. When making this decision, the business considers when its competitors might introduce their new model.
    - All the independent sellers of tourist t-shirts agree to charge $10 each for their t-shirts.

Chapter **8**

Market Failure: Externalities and Public Goods

Under perfect competition, profit-maximizing firms produce the amount of output where price equals marginal cost. When conditions are such that firms are *not* producing this amount of output, economists say there is **market failure**. In the previous chapter, we looked at imperfect competition as a source of market failure. This chapter considers two additional sources of market failure. The first case is externalities, when individuals who are not party to the transaction bear some costs or receive some benefits. The second case is public goods, where someone can consume a product without paying and without impacting their neighbor's ability to consume the same product. In both cases, the amount of output produced in unregulated private markets will not equal the optimum amount.

KEY TERMS AND CONCEPTS

- Market failure
- Negative externality
- Positive externality
- External cost
- Marginal damage cost
- Marginal private costs
- Private marginal costs
- Marginal social cost
- Socially optimal quantity
- Internalizing the externality
- External benefit
- Marginal social benefit
- Social marginal benefit
- Coase theorem
- Private goods
- Rival in consumption
- Excludable
- Public goods

- Nonrival in consumption
- Nonexcludable
- Free rider problem

KEY EQUATIONS

- Marginal social cost
- Marginal social benefit

KEY GRAPHS

- Negative externality
- Positive externality
- Public good

EXTERNALITIES

When Amanda drives her SUV, she pays only some of the costs. Amanda pays for the gas, oil, tolls, parking, and any car taxes. But she doesn't pay for the carbons her car releases into the air, the congestion her car adds to traffic, nor the asthma attacks her exhaust triggers. This is an example of what economists call a **negative externality**. When some of the costs of an activity are borne by individuals who are not directly involved in the activity, the people undertaking the activity—Amanda, in our example—are generating negative externalities. Common examples are pollution and global warming.

When Josiah paints his house, he receives only some of the benefits. Josiah enjoys the new look of his house and the increase to his property value. But his neighbors also benefit: It is more pleasant to walk by Josiah's house and their property values have also increased. This is an example of what economists call a **positive externality**. When some of the benefits of an activity are received by individuals who are not directly involved in the activity, the people undertaking the activity—Josiah, in our example—are generating positive externalities. Common examples of positive externalities are education and driving hybrid cars.

Negative and positive externalities generate market failure because the private market, left to its own, will produce the wrong quantity. Amanda doesn't take into account the costs of her action on others. She will drive more than society wants her to. In general, the private market produces too much when there are negative externalities.

Josiah doesn't take into account the benefits of his action on his neighbors. He will paint his house less often and spruce up the garden less often than his neighbors would like. In general, the private market produces too little when there are positive externalities.

The usual solution to these problems is government intervention. When negative externalities are present, the government can impose a tax on the activity. When an activity is more expensive, people will do it less.

When there are positive externalities, the government can provide a subsidy, making the activity less expensive. The private market will produce more of the activity.

TRY

Answers to all "Try" questions are of the back of the book.

1. In each case below, is the activity generating positive externalities, negative externalities, or no externalities?
   A. A large truck uses its very loud air brakes to slow down as it drives through a residential neighborhood
   B. A high school teacher takes a summer class to increase his knowledge of the subject area and learn new teaching methods
   C. A woman wears perfume

A GRAPHICAL APPROACH: NEGATIVE EXTERNALITY

Imagine that we could put a dollar price on the climate, congestion, and health effects of Amanda's driving her SUV. For every mile she drives, the climate, congestion, and health effects cost $1. Economists call this cost of a negative externality the **external cost** or the **marginal damage cost**. Both phrases are used interchangeably.

Amanda takes into account only her private costs. Economists call those costs her **marginal private costs** or **private marginal costs**. Some textbooks use one phrase; other books use the other.

When Amanda decides how much to drive, she compares simply her marginal private costs and her marginal benefit. She will drive the number of miles where her marginal benefit equals her marginal cost. In Figure 8.1, we label that q_P for private optimal quantity.

The rest of us want Amanda to take into account the climate, congestion, and health effects of her driving. The true total cost per mile of Amanda's driving is captured not just by her marginal private costs. The true total cost—the cost to Amanda *and* the rest of us—is the sum of her marginal private costs and the marginal damage cost. Economists call that total the **marginal social cost**.

Marginal social cost = marginal private cost + marginal damage cost

The **socially optimal quantity** will be the quantity where marginal benefit equals marginal *social* cost. In Figure 8.1, the socially optimal quantity is labeled q_S. In the presence of negative externalities, the socially optimal quantity is lower than the private optimal quantity.

A self-interested individual has no incentive to change their behavior just because it negatively affects hundreds or thousands of strangers. Without intervention, the private market will continue to produce too much of an activity, which itself produces negative externalities.

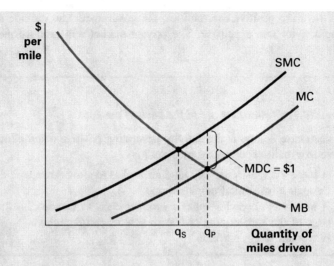

Figure 8.1 Negative externality.
The private optimal quantity is q_P, where private marginal benefit (MB) equals private marginal cost (MC). The socially optimal quantity takes into account the marginal damage cost, which here is $1 per mile driven. The socially optimal quantity is q_S where marginal benefit (MB) equals social marginal cost (SMC).

How can we get Amanda to take into account the climate, congestion, and health effects of her driving? If the government imposes a tax on Amanda's driving, she will take this cost into account when determining how much to drive. If the tax equals the marginal damage cost, Amanda will then drive the socially optimal number of miles, q_S. In general, to force markets that generate negative externalities to produce a socially optimal quantity, the government can impose a tax or penalty equal to the marginal damage cost. Economists would say that Amanda is now **internalizing the externality**.

In most cases, the tax reduces but does not eliminate the offending behavior. But if the marginal damage cost is so great that there is no point where Amanda's private marginal benefit equals or exceeds the marginal social cost, a well-designed tax will eliminate the behavior that creates the negative externality.

TRY

2. What is the difference between marginal private cost and marginal social cost?

3. In the presence of negative externalities, why is the private optimum quantity larger than the socially optimum quantity?

4. If the marginal damage cost of driving while talking on a cell phone is $10 per occurrence, then what penalty would be the optimal penalty for this activity?

A GRAPHICAL APPROACH: POSITIVE EXTERNALITY

The approach to a positive externality is similar. Amanda is considering trading in her SUV for a hybrid. Imagine that we could put a dollar value on the climate and health benefits of driving a hybrid. For every mile that Amanda drives her hybrid, the beneficial side effects are valued at $2. This is a benefit of Amanda's activity that the rest of us enjoy. Economists call this an **external benefit**.

Again, Amanda takes into account just her private benefit and private cost. She effectively undervalues the marginal benefit of driving a hybrid because she is not taking into account the climate and health benefits for the rest of us. Amanda will buy and drive a hybrid if her private marginal benefit of doing so exceeds her private marginal cost. Amanda's private optimum is shown by q_P in Figure 8.2.

The rest of us want Amanda to take into account the beneficial side effects of owning a hybrid. We want Amanda to take into account both her private marginal benefit *and* the external benefit. The total is called **marginal social benefit** or **social marginal benefit**. Some books use one phrase; some use the other.

Marginal social benefit = private marginal benefit + external benefit

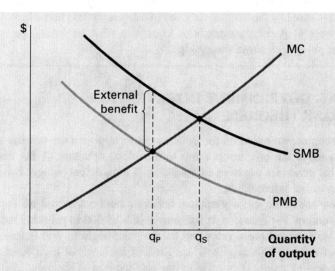

Figure 8.2 Positive externality.
The private optimal quantity is q_P where private marginal benefit (PMB) equals marginal cost (MC). But in the presence of positive externalities, the social marginal benefit (SMB) exceeds the private marginal benefit. The socially optimal quantity is q_S, where social marginal benefit equals marginal cost.

The socially optimal quantity is the quantity where marginal social benefit equals marginal cost. In Figure 8.2, the socially optimal quantity is labeled q_S. In the presence of positive externalities, the socially optimal quantity is greater than the private optimal quantity.

A self-interested individual has no incentive to take positive externalities into account. We can cajole, persuade, argue, advertise. Altruistic individuals may be moved by concern for the environment to change their behavior. But in general, so long as the private benefit falls short of the social benefit, the private optimum will fall short of the social optimum.

How can we persuade Amanda to trade in her SUV for an environmentally-friendly car? Again, the government can play a role. If the government offers a subsidy equal to the external benefit of the hybrid, Amanda's private optimum will equal the social optimum. She will choose to drive more with the hybrid than with the SUV. Again, economists would say Amanda has internalized the externality.

TRY

5. The external benefit of a teacher taking a summer class in her field is $3,000 per class. If teachers have to pay for the entire class themselves, will the optimal private quantity equal the socially optimal quantity? What is the optimal size of the subsidy?

6. Homeowners get a federal income tax break. They can reduce the income that is taxed by the amount they pay in interest on their home loan. Use the concept of positive externalities to explain why the federal government thus subsidizes home ownership.

AVOIDING GOVERNMENT INTERVENTION: THE COASE THEOREM

In both examples, we relied on the government to impose a tax or offer a subsidy in order to move the private optimum to the social optimum. A tax discourages behavior that generates negative externalities. A subsidy encourages behavior that generates positive externalities.

In a few cases, the socially optimal behavior can be achieved without government intervention. For example, it will cost Josiah $5,000 to paint his house. He is willing to wait several more years and let the paint begin to peel before spending that kind of money. The neighbors are tired of looking out their front windows and seeing peeling paint. They offer to pay half the cost of the paint job. In effect, they have offered Josiah a subsidy. He will get the house painted sooner than he would have without their offer.

Marissa practices her drums four hours each day, starting at 6:00 A.M. You work until 11:00 P.M. and want to sleep until 8:00 A.M. You value your sleep and are willing to pay up to $40 a day for peace and quiet. Marissa needs to practice but can be persuaded—for a small fee of $25 per day—to wait until 8:00 A.M. You offer Marissa $25 per day. You get more sleep; Marissa postpones her practice. No government intervention was needed.

Josiah's paint job and Marissa's drum practice are examples where private negotiation solves the externality problem. Several conditions must exist for private negotiation to be successful.

- There must be relatively few parties to the transaction. You and your neighbor can work something out. Amanda and everyone affected by climate change cannot.

- There must be well-defined and agreed upon property rights. Josiah has the right to paint or not paint his house. Your neighbor has the right to play her drums. There is no property right to the view of the neighborhood, or to quiet.

- There must be no impediments to bargaining. Hiring expensive lawyers could be an impediment. A lack of trust between neighbors could be an impediment. But if Josiah and his neighbors get along well and trust each other, there are no impediments to bargaining.

If these conditions are satisfied, then government intervention is not needed to bring the private optimum in line with the social optimum. Instead, the parties can negotiate an agreement. This result is called the **Coase theorem** for the man who conceptualized it, Ronald Coase.

TRY

7. For each situation below, does the Coase theorem apply? If not, why not?
   A. Big trucks are using their very loud air brakes as they drive through your neighborhood.
   B. Your neighbor's tree overhangs your house and its debris clogs your drainage system. Your neighbor is a bully who refuses to talk with you.
   C. Your little sister's high school teacher sometimes takes professional development classes during the summer break.
   D. Someone who lives in your apartment complex sweeps the walkways each morning, but only in front of his apartment. You wish he would sweep in front of your apartment too.

PUBLIC GOODS

Up until now, all of the goods or services we've considered are **private goods**. A private good has two characteristics: (1) when you consume a private good, no one else can consume the same private good and (2) you have some way to prevent others from consuming the good if you want to.

As you read and highlight this book, no one else can read and highlight the same copy of the book at the same time. Economists say: A private good is

rival in consumption because your use or consumption of the good prevents—rivals—others from consuming the exact same item at the same time.

You can prevent others from reading the book simply by keeping it in your book bag or on your desk. Economists say: A private good is **excludable** because you can exclude others from consuming it.

There are some products that satisfy neither characteristic. These products are called **public goods**. A public good has two characteristics: (1) when you consume a public good, I can consume the same public good at the same time with no impact on your ability to consume the good and (2) you cannot prevent me from consuming the good.

TIP

The name public *good* is a bit misleading. Almost every public "good" is actually a *service*. Nonetheless, economists use the phrase "public good."

When I listen to a radio station, you can listen to the same radio station at the same time. Economists say: A public good is **nonrival in consumption** because consumption of the good (usually, a service) by one individual does not preclude anyone else from also consuming the good.

When police patrols keep a neighborhood free of burglaries, everyone is made safe. We can't exclude some individuals but not others from the benefits of the police car driving down the street. Economists say: A public good is **nonexcludable** because no one can be excluded from consuming the good.

An unregulated private market will not produce the socially optimal quantity of a public good. This is because self-interested individuals have no incentive to pay for public goods. Economists say: Public goods suffer from the **free rider problem**. Self-interested individuals can "free ride" on the generosity of others. Once the public good is produced, free riders can consume the good without paying because their consumption cannot be prevented. But if everyone is self-interested and thus no one is willing to pay, the public good won't be produced at all.

Some public goods are produced by the private market because not everyone is motivated purely by self-interest. Public radio and public television are good examples. Public radio stations are generally FM stations at the left end of the dial, which provide news, arts, and cultural programming. Public television brings us programs such as *Sesame Street* and *Between the Lions*. Public radio and television stations in the United States conduct fundraising drives several times a year. The station operators interrupt programming and ask listeners to call in and contribute money to keep the station on the air. The station announcers will say "Only 1 in 7 listeners to this station is a current contributor." That means 6 out of 7 listeners are free-riding on the generosity of others.

Depending on the generosity of others works for public radio and television. But it wouldn't work for all public goods. The usual solution is for the government to tax all who benefit from the public good and to then provide the good. The dilemma the government faces is how much to produce.

Table 8.1 How Much Would You Pay for a Public Good?

# drives through neighborhood	How much would you pay for that drive through the neighborhood?			
	Sarah	Diego	Taylor	You
1	$10	$12	$5	$6
2	7	4	3	4
3	5	0	1	2
4	2	0	0	0
5	0	0	0	0

When the police drive down your street at night, their presence protects you from burglaries. How many times a night should the police drive down your street? The answer depends on the marginal benefit that you and your neighbors receive from the police patrol and on the marginal cost of those patrols. The socially optimal quantity of any good is the quantity where the social marginal benefit equals the social marginal cost.

How do we value the marginal benefit? The marginal benefit is burglaries prevented. But we can't compare the *number* of burglaries prevented with the *dollar* cost of patrols. We first need to evaluate marginal benefit and marginal cost in the same terms—dollars. What is the *dollar* benefit of the police patrols?

You and your neighbors each receive a survey. How much are you willing to pay per night if the police drive through your neighborhood once, twice, three times? Your answers describe how much you value police protection. Your neighbor Sarah is willing to pay $10 for the police patrol's first drive through the neighborhood, $7 for the second, $5 for the third, $2 for the fourth, and thinks anything beyond four times a night is unnecessary. Another neighbor has a different willingness to pay. And yours is different still. Table 8.1 shows the survey results.

What is the total marginal benefit to the neighborhood? The answer is found by summing the individual marginal benefits. Add across the rows. The marginal benefit to the neighborhood of the police driving through one time per night is $10 + $12 + $5 + $6 = $33. The marginal benefit of the second drive through the neighborhood per night is $7 + $4 + $3 + $4 = $18. The marginal benefit of the third pass through is $5 + $0 + $1 + $2 = $8. The marginal benefit of the fourth drive through is just $2. And there is no marginal benefit to a fifth drive through the neighborhood per night.

TIP

With public goods, total demand is the sum of the amount each individual would pay for some quantity of the good. Add up the dollars for public goods. With private goods, total demand is the sum of the quantity each individual would purchase at some price of the good. Add up the quantities for private goods.

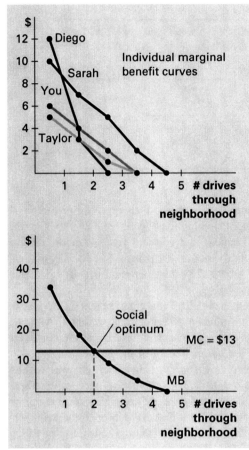

Figure 8.3 Public goods.
The total marginal benefit curve for a public good is the sum, for each quantity, of the individual marginal benefit curves. The socially optimal quantity of output is the output where total marginal benefit (MB) equals marginal cost (MC).

How many times should the police patrol the neighborhood per night? The answer depends on the comparison of marginal benefit and marginal cost. Suppose the marginal cost is $13 per drive through the neighborhood. Then the police should drive through the neighborhood twice per night. If instead the marginal cost was $5 per drive, the patrol should come through three times per night.

Figure 8.3 illustrates. The total marginal benefit in the bottom panel is found by summing vertically the individual marginal benefit curves in the top panel. The socially optimal quantity is where total marginal benefit equals marginal cost.

TRY

8. For each activity below, is it rival or nonrival in consumption? Is it excludable or nonexcludable?

A. A concert in a very large public park

B. A concert in an indoor sports arena

   C. A beautiful sunset

   D. A broadcast on HBO

   E. Military protection

9. What is a free rider?

10. A small town has a church building that is large enough to seat everyone in town. Everyone is welcome to attend the church. However, there is no resident preacher. The townspeople can hire a circuit rider—a preacher who comes to town one, two, three, or four Sundays per month. The preacher asks for $300 per Sunday. Someone surveys the townspeople and finds their willingness to pay is as follows:

- 10 people are willing to pay $10 each for the first visit per month, $5 each for a second visit in a month, $2 each for a third visit in a month, and are unwilling to pay for a fourth visit in a month
- 40 people are willing to pay $5 each for the first visit per month, $1 each for a second visit in a month, and are unwilling to pay for a third or fourth visit in a month
- 30 people are willing to pay $5 each for the first visit per month, but are unwilling to pay anything else.

For how many Sundays per month will the townspeople hire the circuit rider?

Chapter 9

Factor Markets

How many workers does a business hire? How much does an acre of land sell for? How many machines does a business purchase? These are questions about the markets for the factors of production: labor, land, and physical capital. The answers draw upon the supply and demand model, but with slight twists of language. And the roles have switched: Businesses are the buyers who demand factors of production; households are the sellers who supply factors of production. Let's look at each of these three markets in turn: labor, land, and physical capital.

KEY TERMS AND CONCEPTS

- Labor supply
- Labor–leisure tradeoff
- Wage
- Opportunity cost of leisure
- Foregone wages
- The substitution effect
- The income effect
- Backward-bending supply curve
- Labor supply curve
- Marginal revenue product of labor (MRP)
- Marginal physical product of labor (MPP)
- Derived demand
- Marginal revenue product curve
- Labor demand curve
- Equilibrium or market wage
- Equilibrium wage
- Labor surplus
- Labor shortage
- Land supply curve
- Marginal revenue product of the land
- Physical capital
- Buildings
- Machinery
- Equipment or producer durable goods

- Marginal revenue product of capital
- Price of capital
- Expected rate of return
- Interest rates
- Investment decision rule
- Investment spending
- External finance
- Internal finance
- Investment demand curve
- Investment spending
- Optimism
- Pessimism

KEY EQUATIONS

- Marginal revenue product
- Investment decision rule

KEY GRAPHS

- Labor market equilibrium
- Land market
- Investment demand

LABOR MARKETS

Demand and supply was introduced in Chapter 3. What determines the price of spiral notebooks? Demand and supply. The demand for spiral notebooks captures the behavior of buyers of notebooks. At a higher price, there is a lower quantity demanded. The demand curve slopes down. The supply of spiral notebooks captures the behavior of sellers of notebooks. At a higher price, there is a higher quantity supplied. The supply curve slopes up. When the market for spiral notebooks is in equilibrium, spiral notebooks sell for a price where quantity demanded equals quantity supplied.

Labor markets function much the same as markets for spiral notebooks. There is a downward-sloping demand curve and an upward-sloping supply curve. The market price is at the intersection of demand and supply. The language is different; the explanations are different. But the basic logic of supply and demand still applies.

LABOR SUPPLY

Labor is supplied by people. Labor is our time. We offer (sell) some of our time to firms in exchange for money. Economists call this **labor supply**.

There are 24 hours in a day, 7 days in a week. We each decide how we want to allocate our time between working for pay and other activities. Economists call this the **labor–leisure tradeoff**. They use "leisure" to describe all activities that are not work-for-pay, from sleeping to changing diapers to hanging out with friends to volunteering in New Orleans.

What matters most to the labor–leisure tradeoff? The wage we could earn by working. The **wage** is the special name that economists give to the price of labor. The wage is the price we are paid for "selling" one hour of our labor to an employer.

When wages rise, we are torn between supplying more labor and supplying less. When we don't work, we don't get paid. The wage measures the cost of not working. Economists say: The **opportunity cost of leisure** is the **foregone wages** we could have earned from working. As the cost of leisure rises, we want to devote less time to leisure and more time to working. We could also say: As the wage rises, we substitute working for leisure. Economists call this the **substitution effect** of higher wages: At a higher wage, we want to supply more labor because labor's substitute, leisure, has become more expensive.

At the same time, a higher wage means we earn more income for the same number of hours of work. Working 20 hours per week gives us $200 in income at $10 per hour but fully $300 in income at $15 per hour. As our income rises, we want to consume more of any normal good. Leisure is a normal good. So as income rises, demand for leisure increases. Economists call this **the income effect** of higher wages: At a higher wage, we want to supply less labor because our income allows us to consume more leisure.

TIP

Remember from Chapter 3: A normal good is something we want to buy *more* of when our income rises.

The substitution effect says the quantity of labor supplied *rises* as wages rise because leisure has become pricier. The income effect says the quantity of labor supplied *falls* as wages rise because leisure has become more affordable. Which effect is larger? At all but the highest wage, the substitution effect dominates: An increase in wages calls forth an increase in the quantity of labor supplied. At very high wages—higher than most of us can expect to see in our lifetimes—the income effect dominates: An increase in wages results in a smaller quantity of labor supplied. Economists call this unusual result a **backward-bending supply curve**.

Figure 9.1 illustrates the **labor supply curve**. Over most of the range of wages, the labor supply curve is upward sloping. At very high wages, the labor supply curve is downward sloping or "bends backward."

TRY

Answers to all "Try" questions are at the back of the book

   1. What is the substitution effect of an increase in wages? What is the income effect of an increase in wages?

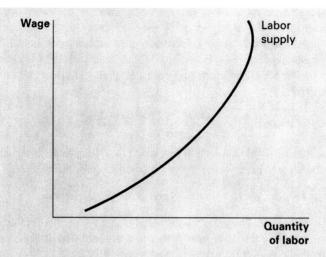

Figure 9.1 Labor supply curve.

The labor supply curve shows how the total number of worker hours (number of workers times number of hours) rises as wages rise ... usually. At very high wages, the labor supply curve "bends backward" because at very high wages, people want to work less, not more, as wages continue to rise.

LABOR DEMAND

Labor is demanded by firms or businesses. A business hires workers in order to produce output, which the business sells to its customers. What determines how many workers a business wants to hire, and for how many hours? The wage the business must pay to the workers matters, of course. But also businesses care about how much output the workers can produce and what price the business can charge for its output.

A business should hire workers and give them hours so long as the workers' contribution to revenue exceeds the wages paid. If having someone work a 30th hour this week adds $50 revenue to the firm, the business should be willing to pay that worker up to $50. But if working the 31st hour adds just $5 revenue to the firm, the business should pay no more than $5 to have someone work that 31st hour in a week.

Economists call the worker's contribution to revenue the **marginal revenue product of labor**, or **MRP**. Some books put a subscript on the notation: MRP_L. The marginal revenue product is the change in total revenue from one additional hour of work.

$$Marginal\ revenue\ product = \frac{Change\ in\ total\ revenue}{Change\ in\ number\ of\ hours\ worked} = \frac{\Delta TR}{\Delta L}$$

In a perfectly competitive market, the business has no control over the price it charges for its output. Businesses in a perfectly competitive market are price takers. The price they charge for output is determined by the market demand and supply.

In this case, the change in total revenue generated by one more hour of labor is just the price of the output multiplied by the amount of output a worker produces in an hour. Economists call the additional output produced by an hour of labor the **marginal physical product of labor** or **MPP**. (Some textbooks simply use MP as shorthand for marginal product, dropping the word "physical".) In a perfectly competitive market,

$$MRP = Price\ of\ output \times \frac{\Delta Quantity\ Produced}{\Delta L} = Price\ of\ output \times MPP$$

A profit-maximizing business will hire workers so long as the marginal revenue product of the worker exceeds the wage the business pays the worker.

Profit-max rule: Hire workers so long as MRP > wage

Because the marginal revenue product depends on the market for the business's output, economists say the demand for labor is a **derived demand**. Labor demand is derived from the demand for the business s output.

How many workers will a firm hire and for how many hours a week? The answer depends on the marginal revenue product of the workers. The firm is in a perfectly competitive industry. It cannot influence the wage rate. So the firm takes the wage as given. "Workers are being paid $12 per hour in this town, so we will also need to pay $12 per hour."

TIP

Remember—the law of diminishing returns tells us that as the number of workers in a firm is increased, their marginal product will decrease.

The more workers the firm hires, the lower the marginal product of the last worker. So the **marginal revenue product curve** slopes down. Figure 9.2 shows an individual firm's demand for labor. When the wage is $12 per hour, this firm will employ workers for 200 hours per week. Perhaps this is 10 workers for 20 hours each, or 5 workers for 40 hours each. Either way, the employer will be paying for 200 hours of labor each week.

The marginal revenue product curve is the individual firm's labor demand curve. At a wage higher than $12 per hour, the firm employs workers for fewer than 200 hours each week. Why? The key is the law of diminishing returns. When the firm employs workers for fewer hours, the marginal product of labor will rise due to the law of diminishing returns. So at a higher wage, the firm cuts back on how many workers it employs until the marginal revenue product rises to equal the higher wage. At a wage below $12 per hour, the firm employs additional workers.

The total market demand for labor is simply the sum of each individual firm's marginal revenue product. The law of diminishing returns tells us the marginal revenue product curves all slope down. And so the **labor demand curve** slopes down also.

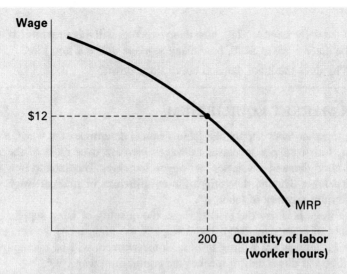

Figure 9.2 Marginal revenue product of labor.

As more workers are employed, the marginal revenue product (MRP) of the last worker declines due to the law of diminishing returns. A business wants to maximize profit, so it will hire additional workers only if the MRP of the last worker hired is at least as great as the wage. Here, the firm will want to employ 200 worker-hours at a wage of $12 per hour. At a higher wage, the firm will demand a smaller quantity of labor. At a lower wage, the firm will demand a greater quantity of labor.

TRY

2. What is the definition of the marginal revenue product of labor? For perfectly competitive firms, what is the connection between the marginal revenue product of labor and the price of the firm's output?

3. Why does the marginal product of labor decline (or, diminish) as the quantity of labor employed increases? (You may need to look back at a previous chapter to answer this one!)

4. Complete the table below.

# Workers	Total Product per day	Marginal Product	Marginal Revenue Product When Output Sells for $6
0	0		
1	50		
2	90		
3	120		
4	140		

If the daily wage is $240, how many workers will this firm hire? If instead the daily wage is $280, how many workers will the firm hire?

5. Why does the labor demand curve slope down?

LABOR MARKET EQUILIBRIUM

Bringing together labor supply and labor demand determines the wage. Figure 9.3 illustrates. Labor supply increases as wages increase over most of the range of wages. Labor demand decreases as wages increase. The intersection of labor supply and labor demand determines the **equilibrium** or **market wage**, w*, and the equilibrium quantity of labor, q*.

If the wage is above the market wage, the quantity of labor supplied exceeds the quantity of labor demanded. If the wage is too high, more workers will want jobs than businesses are willing to hire. Some workers will be unemployed. The wage will be bid down until it reaches the equilibrium wage, w*.

If the wage is below the market wage, the quantity of labor supplied will be less than the quantity of labor demanded. If the wage is too low, businesses will want to hire more workers than are available. There will be lots of "Help Wanted" signs and job listings. The wage will be bid up until it reaches the **equilibrium wage**, w*.

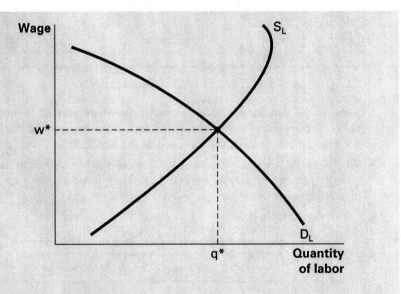

Figure 9.3 Labor market equilibrium.

The labor market is in equilibrium when the quantity of labor demanded equals the quantity of labor supplied. Here, the equilibrium wage is w* and the equilibrium quantity of labor is q*.

Changes of Labor Market Equilibrium

It is important to know the difference between *movements along* and *shifts of* the supply and demand curves. Any time the wage changes, there is a movement along a curve. If anything else that affects labor supply or labor demand changes, the entire curve shifts.

Shifts of Labor Supply

The labor supply curve captures the labor–leisure tradeoff of workers. A change in tastes or in institutions that alters our desire to work can shift the labor supply curve. More white married women entered the U.S. labor force in the 1970s. Political movements, legal changes, and other causes lay behind the increase. The labor supply curve shifted to the right.

In general, if more workers join the economy, the labor supply curve shifts to the right. If workers leave the economy, the labor supply curve shifts to the left.

An increase in labor supply—a shift to the right of the labor supply curve—lowers the equilibrium wage. Figure 9.4a illustrates. At the old wage, the quantity of labor supplied now exceeds the quantity of labor demanded. There is a **labor surplus**: unemployment. Wages will be bid down.

A decrease in labor supply—a shift to the left of the labor supply curve—raises the equilibrium wage. Figure 9.4b illustrates. At the old wage, the quantity of labor supplied is now less than the quantity of labor demanded. There is a **labor shortage**. Wages will be bid up.

Shifts of Labor Demand

The labor demand curve came from the marginal revenue product curves of each firm. Remember: Marginal revenue product of labor in competitive industries equals

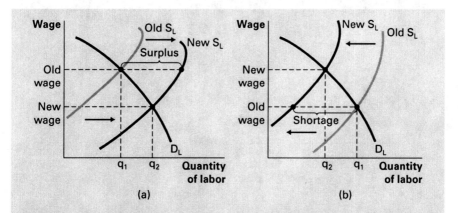

Figure 9.4 Shift of labor supply.

When labor supply increases as in Figure 9.4a, there is a labor surplus at the old wage. As a result, the equilibrium wage declines and equilibrium quantity of labor rises. When labor supply decreases as in Figure 9.4b, there is a labor shortage at the old wage. As a result, the equilibrium wage rises and the equilibrium quantity of labor declines.

marginal physical product of labor times the price of the output. So labor demand reflects how productive workers are and how much is charged for the product they are producing. A change in worker productivity or in output prices changes the workers' marginal revenue product. The labor demand curve will shift.

If workers become more productive—able to produce more output in an hour—then firms will be willing to pay higher wages. Labor demand increases.

If the price of the good or service the workers are producing rises, then again firms will be willing to pay higher wages. Labor demand increases.

An increase in labor demand shifts the labor demand curve to the right. At every wage, firms are willing to hire more workers. Figure 9.5a illustrates. At the old wage, the quantity of labor demanded now exceeds the quantity of labor supplied. There is a shortage of labor. Firms are looking for workers. Wages will be bid up.

TIP

Notice that a shift to the right of the labor demand curve looks the same as a shift *up* of the labor demand curve. The intuition is often easier if you think of the labor demand curve as shifting up: an increase in how much employers are willing to pay to workers.

A decrease in labor demand shifts the labor demand curve to the left. At every wage, firms will hire fewer workers. Figure 9.5b illustrates. At the old wage, the quantity of labor supplied now exceeds the quantity of labor demanded. There is a surplus of labor. Workers are unemployed. Wages will fall.

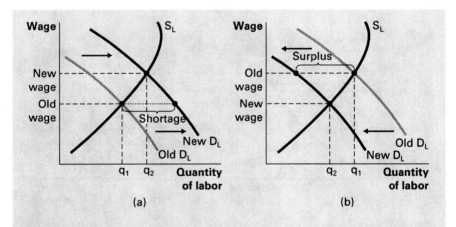

Figure 9.5 Shift of labor demand.

When the demand for labor increases as in Figure 9.5a, there is a labor shortage at the old wage. As a result, the equilibrium wage rises and the equilibrium quantity of labor also rises. When the demand for labor decreases as in Figure 9.5b, there is a labor surplus at the old wage. As a result, the equilibrium wage falls and the equilibrium quantity of labor also falls.

TRY

6. For each scenario described below, decide whether there is a change in labor demand or labor supply. Do wages rise or fall? Does employment rise or fall?

   A. Increased popularity of computer science as a college major increases the number of people entering the computer industry.
   B. Prices of fresh fruit decline, affecting the market for fruit pickers.
   C. A new way of organizing workers in the workplace raises the productivity of manufacturing workers.
   D. The price of clothing increases, affecting the market for retail salespeople.

7. Here again is the table from "TRY" question #4.

# Workers	Total Product per Day	Marginal Product	Marginal Revenue Product When Output Sells for $6	Marginal Revenue Product When Output Sells for $8
0	0			
1	50			
2	90			
3	120			
4	140			

The daily wage is $240. How many workers will the firm hire if output sells for $6 each? How many workers will the firm hire if instead output sells for $8?

MISUSE OF THE LABOR MARKET MODEL

When we studied supply and demand in Chapter 3, we were sure to carefully define the market for the product. Equilibrium was defined not for "school supplies" generally, nor "office products" even more generally, but for "spiral notebooks" in particular.

So too with the labor market model. We need to carefully define the market. Are we looking at the market for sales clerks in women's clothing stores? For physics professors at research universities? For restroom custodians at a major sports venue? The introduction of computer-readable bar codes on sales tags at Target increased the productivity of Target's sales clerks, but did nothing to alter the productivity of the people hosing down the men's room at Fenway Park in Boston.

A common misuse of the labor market model is to lump together all the workers in the economy. Labor demand is then defined as the total demand for workers in the entire economy. Labor supply is then defined as the total supply of workers in the entire economy. But these definitions are a misuse of the labor market model. There is too much movement between the various labor markets for lumping everyone together to truly make much sense.

The labor market model helps us understand changes in wages, so long as we carefully define the labor market we are studying. How did the entry of married white women into the labor force in the 1970s affect the market for physics professors at major research universities? It didn't. But their entry did impact the markets for office workers and teachers. Always carefully define the market you are studying.

LAND MARKETS

What determines the price of an acre of land? **Land** is also an input, a factor of production. So the same concepts used to study labor are used to study land.

Demand for land depends on the marginal revenue product of an acre of land. How much revenue does one more acre of land add? An acre of land in Manhattan adds much more revenue to a developer's business than does an acre of land in the middle of Mississippi.

Supply of land? It is what it is! Aside from landfill increasing acreage or rising oceans decreasing it, the supply of land is fixed. There are 74,240 acres in Omaha, Nebraska, and that number is unlikely to change.

Because the supply of land is fixed, the **land supply curve** is vertical. We know what the equilibrium quantity will be. It will be the quantity of acres in that site. Only one question remains: What price will an acre sell for?

The price of an acre of land depends on the **marginal revenue product of the land**. Whomever can earn the most revenue from the land will be willing to pay the highest price for that land. An acre of land in midtown Manhattan will not generate much revenue for a farmer growing corn. But that same land in Manhattan can generate millions of dollars in revenue for a developer who builds a high-rise building on it. The developer will be willing to pay much more money than a farmer for an acre of land in midtown Manhattan.

At what price will the land sell? It will sell at a price equal to its highest marginal revenue product. The land's marginal revenue product depends in part on the natural productivity of the land due to climate, drainage, and soil type. And its marginal revenue product depends on the price of the output produced on the land.

Figure 9.6 illustrates. Several acres of land in midtown Manhattan is available. That is the supply of land. A corn farmer could grow very little corn on that land; there is very little direct light and asphalt is not conducive to growing corn. The farmer's marginal revenue product for that land is quite low.

A real estate developer could build high-rise buildings on the land. The location is excellent for office and residential buildings. So the developer's marginal revenue product for that land is higher than the farmer's. The land will be sold to the developer, who will be willing to pay a price equal to the marginal revenue product when the land is used for real estate development.

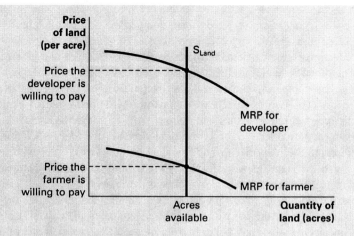

Figure 9.6 Land market.

The supply of land does not change with price, so the supply curve is vertical. The price of an acre of land depends on the land's marginal revenue product (MRP). An acre of land in Manhattan would generate much greater revenue for a real estate developer than it would for a farmer. So the developer's MRP is above the farmer's MRP for that very same acre of land. The land will sell to the developer, who will pay a price equal to the land's marginal revenue product.

TRY

8. Why is the land supply curve vertical?

9. A century ago, there were dairy farms in Berkeley. But today there are none. Use the land market model to explain why there are no longer any farms in Berkeley.

10. Rice requires very wet land in order to grow. Corn rots in very wet land. Why would swampy land be more likely to sell to a rice farmer than to a corn farmer?

MARKETS FOR PHYSICAL CAPITAL

Physical capital is the third input or factor of production. Economists use the phrase "physical capital" to mean **buildings** and **machinery**. Machinery includes more than just machines. Filing cabinets, desks, and computers are also considered machinery. Sometimes machinery is instead called **equipment** or **producer durable goods**.

TIP

Capital does *not* mean stocks and bonds. Economists use the word "capital" in a very particular way. Capital means buildings and machinery.

How much capital will a profit-maximizing firm purchase? You might guess that the answer once again depends on a comparison of the **marginal revenue product of capital** and the **price of capital**. And in one sense, it does.

But economists don't talk about the decision to purchase capital in terms of the capital's marginal revenue product. Instead, a business decides how much capital to purchase by comparing the capital's **expected rate of return** and prevailing **interest rates**. The two approaches—comparing MRP and price of capital, and comparing expected rate of return and interest rate—come to the same conclusion. If purchasing a new display rack is the right decision for Mary's Clothing Shop when comparing the marginal revenue product of the display rack with its price, then it is also the right decision for Mary's Clothing Shop when comparing the expected rate of return of the display rack and the interest rate.

The expected rate of return on capital is a number that compares the cost of buying the capital with the net gain in revenue from using the capital. Remember: "Capital" means machines and buildings, *not* money. The expected rate of return is expressed in percentage terms. The calculation of expected rate of return—when done correctly—is quite complicated. We leave that to the finance experts. We can think of it, though, in simple terms. Mary's Clothing Shop is looking at a new $500 display rack. It is not well made, so at the end of one year it will need to be thrown away. The increase in revenue from buying and using the new rack is $575. The display rack is paid for out of that $575, leaving a gain of $75 for Mary's Clothing Shop. The expected rate of return from buying and using the display rack is $75/$500 = 15%.

Is buying the display rack the right decision? Will it increase profit? The answer depends on interest rates. A profit-maximizing business compares its gain with its cost. The gain is the net increase in revenue from buying and using the capital. Its cost is the cost of borrowing money to buy the capital. If the gain is greater than the cost, buy the capital. If the gain is less than the cost, don't buy the capital.

The profit-maximizing business follows this rule:

> *If the expected rate of return > interest rate, buy the capital*
> *If the expected rate of return < interest rate, do not buy the capital*

Economists sometimes call this the **investment decision rule**. When businesses buy machinery or construct buildings, economists call this **investment spending**.

Which Interest Rate?

When a business borrows money in order to purchase capital, economists say it is using **external finance**. The cost of using external finance is the interest rate the business pays to borrow money.

If Mary's Clothing Shop buys the display rack, it expects to earn $75, which is 15 percent of the $500 cost of the display rack. But if Mary's Clothing Shop must borrow at an interest rate of 18%, its cost is $90, which is 18 percent of $500. If Mary's Clothing Shop must borrow, it should not buy the display rack. The expected gain of 15 percent is less than the interest cost of 18 percent.

What if the business can just pay for the capital by writing a check?

Economists say the business has used **internal finance**. The cost of using internal finance is an *opportunity cost*. It is the foregone interest income the business could have earned.

Mary's Clothing Shop expects to earn 15 percent if it buys a $500 display rack. Mary's Clothing Shop can write a check to pay for the rack. The bank pays Mary's Clothing Shop interest of 3 percent on the checking account balance. The cost of using the $500 to buy the display rack is 3 percent, the foregone interest income. If Mary's Clothing Shop can write a check for the display rack, it should buy the rack. The expected gain of 15 percent is more than the foregone interest income of 3 percent.

TRY

11. What is external finance? What is internal finance?

12. What is the investment decision rule? Is there one rule for external finance and a different rule for internal finance?

13. Your brother owns a dance club. If he buys new sound equipment, he believes more people will come to his club. He estimates an expected rate of return of 8 percent on the sound equipment. Under what circumstances should he buy the new sound equipment?

Investment Demand Curve

At higher interest rates, businesses spend less on purchasing capital. Fewer investment projects—building or machinery purchases—will have expected rates of return in excess of the higher interest rate.

At lower interest rates, businesses spend more on purchasing capital. More investment projects—building or machinery purchases—will have expected rates of return in excess of the lower interest rate.

TIP

Economists use the term "investment" to refer to purchases of physical capital. Do not get confused. "Investment" has nothing to do with stocks, bonds, or other financial assets.

The **investment demand curve** captures the relationship between interest rates and spending on physical capital. Economists call this **investment spending**. Figure 9.7 is an investment demand curve. A change in interest rates *moves us along* an existing investment demand curve. As interest rates fall along the vertical axis, the amount of investment spending rises along the horizontal axis.

The investment demand curve *shifts* if there is a change in the expected rates of return on physical capital. When businesses become more optimistic about the

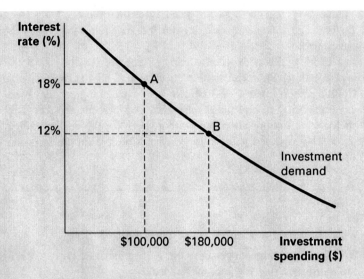

Figure 9.7 Investment demand curve.

An investment demand curve shows how much money businesses will spend on physical capital—machines and buildings—at each interest rate. When interest rates are 18 percent, investment spending is $100,000. This is represented by point A. When interest rates are 10 percent, investment spending is $180,000. This is point B.

future, they think their revenue will rise. **Optimism** makes businesses raise their expected rates of return. The entire investment demand curve shifts to the right.

When businesses become pessimistic about the future, they think their business will not do very well. **Pessimism** makes businesses lower their expected rates of return. The entire investment demand curve shifts to the left.

TRY

14. Interest rates decline. What happens to investment spending? Show this with a graph.

15. The economy enters a downturn. Businesspeople expect sales to decrease over the next several years. If interest rates do not change, what is the effect on investment spending? Show this with a graph.

EPILOGUE

And thus concludes our romp through microeconomics. I hope this little book helped you understand micro a little better!

Answers to "TRY" Questions

CHAPTER 1: ECONOMICS TOOLS: MATH AND GRAPHING

1. $Y = 350 + 0.3Y$
   $0.7Y = 350$
   $Y = 350/0.7 = 500$

2. Rate of change $= (110 - 100)/100$
   $= 10/100 = 0.10 = 10$ percent

3. Rate of change $= (100 - 110)/110 =$
   $-10/110 = -0.091 = -9.1$ percent

4. The rise is negative and the run is positive if we are going from the left to the right. Slope $=$ rise/run $=$ $-2/2 = -1$.

5. Quantity demanded decreases as price increases, so this is a downward-sloping curve.

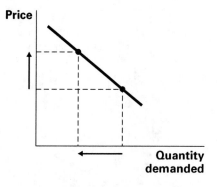

6. Spending increases as wealth increases, but the increases in spending get smaller and smaller as wealth gets larger and larger, so this is a curve with a positive and decreasing slope.

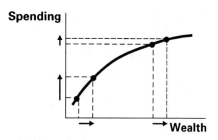

7. As the number of workers increases, their marginal product first increases but then later decreases, so this is a curve that first increases and then decreases.

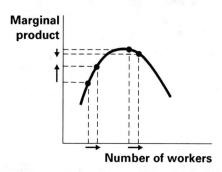

8. Income always equals aggregate spending, so this is a curve with a slope of 1.

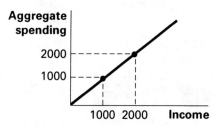

9. When the unemployment rate is low, the inflation rate is high but when the unemployment rate is high, the inflation rate is low, so this is a downward-sloping curve.

10. Quantity supplied increases as price increases, so this is an upward-sloping curve.

11. For a monopolist, as quantity increases, marginal revenue has a steeper negative

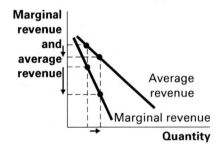

slope than average revenue, so we need two curves, both with a negative slope. The marginal revenue curve will be steeper than the average revenue curve.

12. When the amount of butter produced is decreased from 2,000 to 1,900 units, the number of guns produced increases from 10 to 20 units. But when the amount of butter produced is decreased from 1,000 to 900 units, the number of guns produced increases from 80 to just 82, so this is a curve with a negative and increasing slope (convex to the origin).

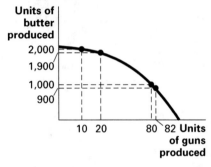

13. Quantity supplied is 13 when price is 5. But when price is 8, quantity supplied is 19. This is an upward-sloping curve.

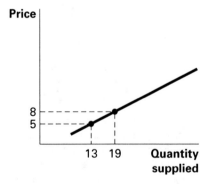

14. When price is 5, quantity demanded is 40. But when price is 10, quantity demanded is 30. This is a downward-sloping curve.

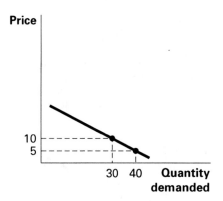

Price

10
5

30 40   **Quantity demanded**

CHAPTER 2: PRODUCTION POSSIBILITIES FRONTIER, ECONOMIC GROWTH, AND GAINS FROM TRADE

1. Opportunity cost of increasing gun production from 15,000 to 20,000 equals 30,000 pounds of butter.

2. Opportunity cost of increasing butter production from 65,000 to 75,000 pounds equals 5,000 guns.

3.

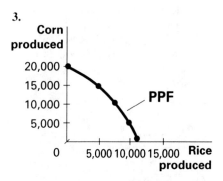

Corn produced

20,000
15,000
10,000
5,000

0   5,000 10,000 15,000   **Rice produced**

PPF

4. Yes, these numbers illustrate the law of increasing opportunity cost. The opportunity cost of increasing rice production rises as the amount of rice that is being produced increases. And the opportunity cost of increasing corn production also rises as the amount of corn that is being produced increases.

5.

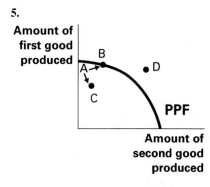

Amount of first good produced

B
A
C
● D

PPF

Amount of second good produced

a. An attainable combination of output is any point *on* the PPF or *inside of* the PPF.

b. An efficient combination of output is any point *on* the PPF.

c. An inefficient combination of output is any point *inside of* the PPF.

d. An unattainable combination of output is any point *above and to the right* of the PPF.

6. No, a combination cannot be simultaneously efficient (using all available resources) and unattainable (impossible to produce with all available resources).

7. Kern County has the absolute advantage in the production of corn; 200 bushels of corn can be produced per acre in Kern County and just 100 bushels per acre can be produced in Taft County.

8. Kern County also has the absolute advantage in the production of wheat; 150 bushels of wheat can be produced per acre in Kern County and just 50 bushels per acre can be produced in Taft County.

9. The "gains from trade" are more output.

10. Yes, Robin and Marian will gain from trading. It does not matter that Robin is better at everything. Robin and Marian will together have a healthier garden and

better meals—gains from trade—if they each specialize in their comparative advantage. Robin should cook and Marian should garden.

CHAPTER 3: DEMAND AND SUPPLY

1. When buyer income rises, demand for normal goods increases. At every price, there is a greater quantity demanded. The entire demand curve shifts to the right. The equilibrium price of laptops will rise. The equilibrium quantity of laptops will also rise.

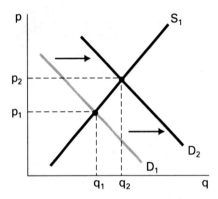

2. When the wages of pen manufacturers rise, this increase in input costs decreases supply of pens. At every price, there is a smaller quantity supplied. The supply curve shifts to the left. The equilibrium price of pens rises. The equilibrium quantity of pens falls.

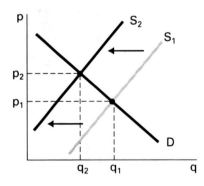

3. When buyer preferences shift toward hybrids, demand for hybrid cars increases. At every price, there is a greater quantity demanded. The entire demand curve shifts to the right. The equilibrium price of hybrid cars will rise. The equilibrium quantity of hybrid cars will also rise.

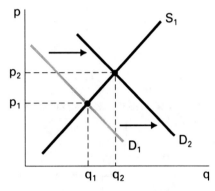

4. When the price of gasoline rises, demand for complementary goods such as SUVs decreases. At every price, there is a smaller quantity demanded. The entire demand curve shifts to the left. The equilibrium price of SUVs will fall. The equilibrium quantity of SUVs will also fall.

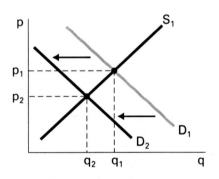

5. When more restaurants open in town, the supply of restaurant meals increases. At every price, there is a greater quantity supplied. The entire supply curve shifts

to the right. The equilibrium price of restaurant meals will fall. The equilibrium quantity of restaurant meals will rise.

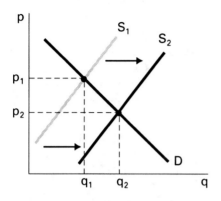

6. When hurricanes destroy dozens of oil rigs, the supply of crude oil decreases. At every price, there is a smaller quantity supplied. The supply curve shifts to the left. The equilibrium price of crude oil rises. The equilibrium quantity of crude oil falls.

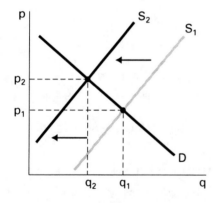

7. When a town's population increases, the demand for rental apartments increases. At every price, there is a greater quantity demanded. The entire demand curve shifts to the right. The equilibrium price of rental apartments will rise. The equilibrium quantity of rental apartments will also rise.

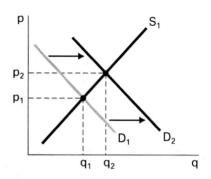

8. When the price of chocolate truffle cookies increases, the supply of brownies decreases. Brownies are substitutes in production for chocolate truffle cookies. At every price, there is a smaller quantity supplied. The supply curve shifts to the left. The equilibrium price of brownies rises. The equilibrium quantity of brownies falls.

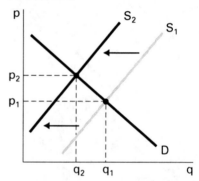

CHAPTER 4: EXTENSIONS OF THE DEMAND AND SUPPLY MODEL

1. The price floor is binding. The quantity sold is less than the equilibrium quantity.

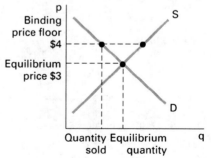

2. The price floor is not binding. The quantity sold is the equilibrium quantity.

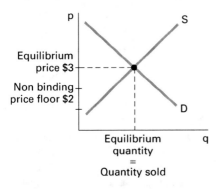

3. The price ceiling is not binding. The quantity sold is the equilibrium quantity.

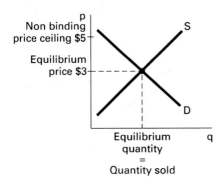

4. The price ceiling is binding. The quantity sold is less than the equilibrium quantity.

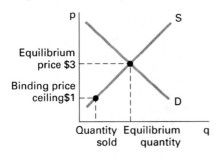

5. Price elasticity of demand $= +8/-10 = -0.8$. Demand is inelastic.

6. Price elasticity of demand $= -3/3 = -1.0$. Demand is unitarily elastic.

7. Price elasticity of demand $= -5/1 = -5.0$. Demand is elastic.

8. Price elasticity of demand $= -\infty/+5 = -\infty$. Demand is perfectly elastic.

9. Price elasticity of demand $= 0/-2 = 0$. Demand is perfectly inelastic.

10. Price elasticity of demand $=$
$$\frac{\left(\dfrac{95-100}{(95+100/2)}\right)}{\left(\dfrac{6-5}{(6+5/2)}\right)} = \frac{-0.051}{+0.182} = -0.28$$

11. Price elasticity of demand $=$
$$\frac{\left(\dfrac{500-2,000}{(500+2,000/2)}\right)}{\left(\dfrac{10-5}{(10+5/2)}\right)}$$
$$= \frac{-1.20}{+0.667} = -1.8$$

12. Price elasticity of demand $=$
$$\frac{\left(\dfrac{11,000-10,000}{(11,000+10,000/2)}\right)}{\left(\dfrac{7-8}{(7+8/2)}\right)}$$
$$= \frac{+0.095}{-0.133} = -0.71$$

13. Total revenue rises when prices are raised and demand is inelastic.

14. Total revenue falls when prices are raised and demand is elastic.

15. Total revenue rises when prices are cut and demand is elastic.

CHAPTER 5: CONSUMER THEORY

1. Because not helping Grandma at all gives you zero (0) satisfaction (that's an assumption economists make), the marginal utility of the first hour of helping your grandmother is $100 - 0 = 100$ utils. The marginal utility of the second hour of helping her is $180 - 100 = 80$ utils.

2. The utility maximization rule is: allocate your spending so that, when you spend your last dollar, MU/P is equal for all goods.

3. To maximize utility when spending $15, buy one jicama, three bags of kettle corn, and four pieces of licorice.

Jicama ($2 each)			Kettle corn ($3 each)			Licorice ($1 each)		
Quantity (Q_J)	Total utility (TU_J)	Marginal utility per dollar (MU_J/P_J)	Quantity (Q_K)	Total utility (TU_K)	Marginal utility per dollar (MU_K/P_K)	Quantity (Q_L)	Total utility (TU_L)	Marginal utility per dollar (MU_L/P_L)
1	80	**40**	1	180	60	1	80	80
2	120	20	2	330	50	2	140	60
3	140	10	3	420	**30**	3	185	45
4	150	5	4	480	20	4	210	**25**
5	156	3	5	510	10	5	230	20

4. When the price of apples increases to $1.50, the MU/P changes, as shown in the fourth column of the table. To maximize utility when spending $20, we should now buy just two apples and 3-3/5 pounds of beef.

Quantity of apples (Q_A)	Total utility from apples	Marginal utility per dollar when $P_A = \$1$ $(MU_A/\$1)$	Marginal utility per dollar when $P_A = \$1.50$ $(MU_A/\$1.50)$	Quantity (pounds) of beef (Q_B)	Total utility from beef	Marginal utility per dollar when $P_B = \$5$ $(MU_B/\$5)$
1	50	50	33.33	1	1,000	200
2	90	40	**26.67**	2	1,800	160
3	115	25	16.67	3	2,025	**45**
4	137	22	14.67	4	2,125	20
5	158	21	14.00	5	2,175	10

5.

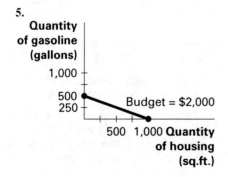

6. The slope of the budget line is $-P_{housing}/P_{gasoline} = -2/4 = -1/2$.

7. When the monthly budget increases to $3,000, the budget line moves out (up and to the right). The slope does not change because the prices have not changed.

8.

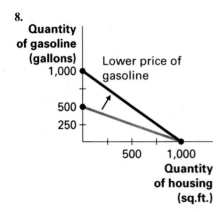

9. We don't know exactly where to draw the second indifference curve for combinations of gasoline and housing that provide 800 utils of satisfaction. But we know it is further from the origin than the indifference curve for combinations that provide 500 utils of satisfaction. So your graph will look something like this.

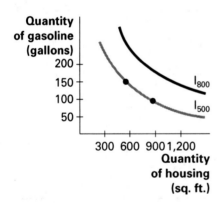

10. The slope of an indifference curve between any two points is the negative of the ratios of the marginal utilities of the two items. In #9, the slope equals $-MU_{housing}/MU_{gasoline}$.

11. The slope of an indifference curve changes—becomes closer and closer to zero—as you move along an indifference curve from upper left to lower right.

12. An indifference curve is convex to the origin and not just a straight line due to the law of diminishing marginal utility.

13.

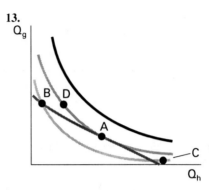

14.

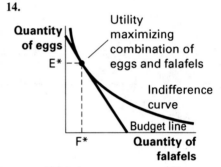

15. When the price of gasoline increases, the budget line pivots down. The quantity of gasoline demanded falls. The demand curve for gasoline does indeed slope down!

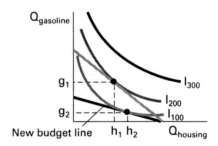

CHAPTER 6: PERFECTLY COMPETITIVE FIRMS

1. The firm's weekly profit is $1,000 because $4,000 − $3,000 = $1,000.

2. Producing an additional 40 pizzas per week will decrease Pepper's Pizza's profit by $100 because the marginal revenue is $400 and the marginal cost is $500. Costs rise more than revenues, so profit falls.

3. The "long run" is the amount of time it takes for a business to sell or buy machinery and buildings, and get out of or enter into any long-run contracts. For Starbucks, a large international chain of coffee shops, it would take them months to sell or buy equipment and storefronts. But an artist who sells paintings at weekend arts and crafts fairs could sell or buy equipment in a matter of days.

4. The marginal product of the 11th worker is $430 - 400 = 30$ pizzas per week. The marginal product of the 12th worker is $455 - 430 = 25$ pizzas per week.

5. Space rental: Fixed cost.
   Electricity bill: Variable cost because it will rise or fall with the number of customers served per month.
   Sinks and styling stations: Fixed cost.
   Insurance: Fixed cost.
   Employees: Variable cost because the employees' hours will vary with the number of customers.
   Shampoo and hair products: Variable cost because the amount of shampoo and hair products used depends on the number of customers.

6. The MC curve intersects the ATC curve at the minimum of the ATC curve.

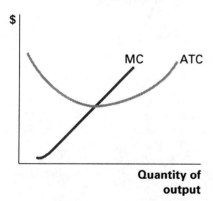

7. The average total cost when output is 100 dolls per day is $2.00 per doll ($2.00 = $200/100$). The average total cost when output is 101 dolls per day is $2.10 per doll ($2.10 = $212.10/101$). The marginal cost of manufacturing the 101st doll is $12.10 = $212.10 - 200.

8. In the short run, when the number of dolls manufactured increases, variable costs increase. Fixed costs do not change as the number of dolls manufactured changes.

9. Zucchini squash sold at the local farmers' market: perfect competition
   Airline flights: oligopoly
   Restaurant meals: monopolistic competition

10.

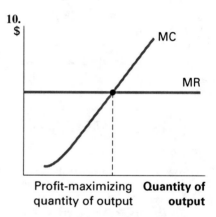

11. When price = p_1, the profit-maximizing quantity of output is 40. When price = p_2, the profit-maximizing quantity of output is 55. When price = p_3, the profit-maximizing quantity of output is 70.

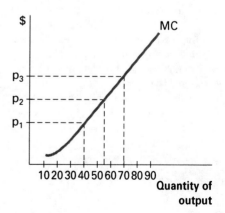

12. Abnormal profit

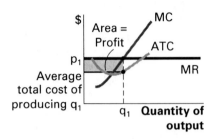

Economic loss

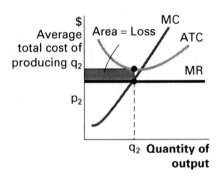

13. The firm is incurring a loss because ATC > price. The dollar amount of the loss is 100 units per day × ($6.00 − $6.50) per unit = $50 per day. In the long run, the firm should exit the industry because it is incurring a loss. In the short run, the firm should continue to produce because the price it's receiving per unit, $6, is greater than the AVC of $4.80. The firm is covering all of its variable costs with its revenue, and covering 100 units × ($6.00 − $4.80) = $120 of its fixed costs per day. The firm loses less by producing than it would by shutting down. But every day, the firm should be trying to sell its equipment and get out of its long-term obligations so it can leave the industry in the long run.

14. The firm is incurring a loss because price < ATC. The loss is 40 units per day × ($75 − $90) per unit = $600 per day. In the long run, the firm should exit the industry because it is incurring a loss. In the short run, the firm should shut down because the price it's receiving per unit, $75, is less than the AVC of $82. The firm loses less by shutting down than it would by producing.

15. No, perfectly competitive firms cannot continue to earn abnormal profit in the long run because new firms will enter the industry, lowering the market price and eroding the abnormal profits earned by the established firms.

CHAPTER 7: IMPERFECT COMPETITION

1.

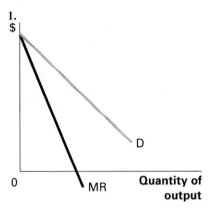

2. The quantity effect is an increase in revenue of $30: ($30 × 101) − ($30 × 100) = $330 − $300 = $30. The price effect is a decrease in revenue of $22: ($28 × 101) − ($30 × 101) = $308 − $300 = − $22. Marginal revenue is +$8 = $30 − $22, or ($28 × 101) − ($30 × 100) = $308 − $300 = $8.

3.

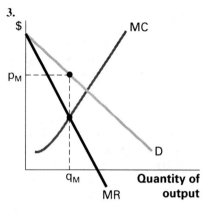

4.

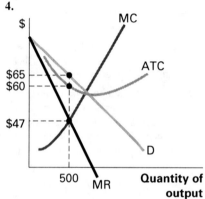

5. Profit = ($65 revenue per unit − $60 average total cost per unit) × 500 units per day = $2, 500 per day

6. Yes, the monopolist can continue to earn abnormal profit in the long run. There are barriers that prevent other firms from entering the industry and competing away the monopolist's profit.

7. Under perfect competition, firms produce identical, indistinguishable products, but under monopolistic competition, firms produce distinguishable products. Under monopoly, barriers to entry prevent other firms from entering the industry, but under monopolistic competition, there are no barriers to entry.

8. The profit-maximizing rule for a firm in a monopolistically competitive industry is to produce the quantity where marginal revenue (MR) equals marginal cost (MC).

9.

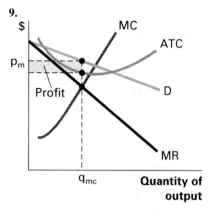

10. In the long run, a typical firm in a monopolistically competitive industry earns zero profit. This is because there are no barriers that prevent other firms from entering the industry. If a typical firm is earning abnormal profit, other firms will enter the industry, take away business from the profitable firm, and the initial firm's economic profit will fall to zero.

11. Earning zero economic profit means doing as well as you could do anywhere else. When economic profit is zero, accounting profit is your opportunity cost—the maximum amount you could earn with your labor and your savings if you were doing something else. If your opportunity cost is $80,000 a year, than zero economic profit means your accounting profit is $80,000 a year. Not bad!

12. Shift the demand and marginal revenue curves in Figure 7.5 to the left in order to get to Figure 7.6's depiction of zero economic profit.

13. The only definitive statement we can make about oligopoly is that profit is maximized by producing the quantity where MR = MC.

14. Fence-building companies: Cournot
Bookstores: Price-leadership
Four companies: Kinked demand
New model: Game theory
Tourist t-shirts: Collusion

CHAPTER 8: MARKET FAILURE: EXTERNALITIES AND PUBLIC GOODS

1. A. Negative externality

   B. Positive externality

   C. Both negative externality (for those with allergies) and positive externality (for those who like the smell)

2. Marginal private cost measures just the cost to the person undertaking the activity and ignores costs borne by others. Marginal social cost includes as well the external or marginal damage cost, which measures the cost to others of someone's activity.

3. The private optimal quantity is larger than the socially optimal quantity in the presence of negative externalities because the private quantity depends on the marginal private cost and not the marginal social cost. The socially optimal quantity depends on the marginal social cost. When there are negative externalities, marginal social cost is greater than marginal private cost. Higher costs lead to smaller quantities.

4. The optimal penalty for driving while talking on a cell phone is the size of the external cost, or $10 per occurrence.

5. If teachers have to pay for the entire class themselves, the optimal private quantity will be less than the socially optimal quantity. In the absence of a subsidy, the teachers would consider only their private benefit and not also the external benefit when deciding how many summer classes to take. The optimal size of the subsidy is $3,000 per class, the amount of the external benefit.

6. The federal government subsidizes home ownership by reducing taxes owed by homeowners. This subsidy is consistent with the idea that home ownership provides society with benefits that don't accrue just to the homeowner. Lower crime and higher political participation are two benefits that many believe are associated with more home ownership.

7. A. No. Too many parties. If there were just one or two truck drivers, then the Coase theorem could apply.

   B. No, the neighbor's bullying behavior represents an impediment to bargaining. If you get along well enough with your neighbor to be able to work something out, then the Coase theorem would apply.

   C. No. Too many parties. The high school teacher works with lots of students every year. Getting all of those students or parents together to try to work out a way to subsidize the teacher's summer classes is unlikely to happen.

   D. Yes. You can talk with your neighbor and ask if you can pay him to sweep in front of your apartment as well.

8. A. Nonrival in consumption (my listening doesn't affect your ability to listen) and nonexcludable (even a rope around the preferred seating area wouldn't prevent me from listening)

   B. Nonrival in consumption and excludable (ticket-takers can be posted at the door, and the sound will not escape the building)

C. Nonrival in consumption (my viewing the sunset doesn't impact your ability to do so) and nonexcludable (anyone can view the sunset)

D. Nonrival in consumption (my watching the broadcast doesn't impact your ability to do so) but excludable (you have to pay your cable or satellite company in order to receive a signal from HBO)

E. Nonrival in consumption (my being protected doesn't diminish your ability to be protected) and nonexcludable (if I am protected from attacks from enemies, then my neighbors are also)

9. A free rider is someone who consumes a public good but doesn't pay for it.

10. The willingness to pay is calculated by adding up the amount the townspeople would collectively pay for each Sunday's visit. For the first visit, 10 people would pay $10 each, and 70 people would pay $5 each, for a total of $450. So the townspeople would be willing to hire the circuit rider for one Sunday a month. For the second visit each month, 10 people would pay $5 each and 40 people would pay $1 each, for a total of $90. The townspeople would not be willing to hire the circuit rider for a second Sunday a month.

CHAPTER 9: FACTOR MARKETS

1. When wages increase, the opportunity cost of leisure increases. So workers substitute away from the now-more-expensive leisure, increasing how much they want to work. This is the substitution effect of an increase in wages. But when wages increase, income increases, and so demand for normal goods increases. Leisure is a normal good, so workers increase how much time they want to allocate to leisure, decreasing how much they want to work. This is the income effect of an increase in wages.

2. The marginal revenue product of labor is the additional revenue to the firm from employing one more worker. For perfectly competitive firms, the marginal revenue product of labor simply equals the price of the firm's output times the marginal physical product of labor.

3. Each additional worker increases total output (marginal product is greater than zero). But each additional worker must share the existing space and machinery with all the other workers. So each additional worker adds less output to the firm than did the previous worker. This is called the law of diminishing marginal returns.

4.

# Workers	Total Product per Day	Marginal Product	Marginal Revenue Product When Output Sells for $6
0	0		
1	50	50	$300
2	90	40	$240
3	120	30	$180
4	140	20	$120

If the daily wage is $240, the firm will hire two workers. It will not hire a third worker because the third worker adds only $180 in revenue to the firm but would cost $240. If instead the daily wage is $280, the firm will hire only one worker. The firm will not hire the second worker because the second worker adds $240 in revenue to the firm, which is less than a daily wage of $280.

5. The labor demand curve slopes down because of the law of diminishing marginal returns. As employment increases, marginal physical product and therefore marginal revenue product decline.

6. A. Increases labor supply in the computer industry. Wages in the computer industry fall while employment rises.

 B. Decreases labor demand in the fresh fruit industry. Wages of fruit pickers fall as does employment.

 C. Increases labor demand for manufacturing workers, raising wages and employment in manufacturing.

 D. Increases labor demand for retail salespeople, raising wages and employment in retail sales.

7.

# Workers	Total Product per Day	Marginal Product	Marginal Revenue Product When Output Sells for $6	Marginal Revenue Product When Output Sells for $8
0	0			
1	50	50	$300	$400
2	90	40	$240	$320
3	120	30	$180	$240
4	140	20	$120	$160

When the daily wage is $240, the firm will hire two workers if output sells for $6 each. But if instead output sells for $8, the firm will hire three workers.

8. The land supply curve is vertical because the amount of land available is what it is. Rising ocean levels can decrease the amount of land. Filling in lakes with landfill can increase the amount of land. But aside from these extremes, the amount of land is what it is. The planet won't increase or decrease in size in response to a change in the price of land.

9. A century ago, dairy farmers in Berkeley could earn good revenue from their cows, and no one could earn more from that land doing anything else. So the dairy farmers owned the land because it was worth more to them than it would be to anyone else. The farmers had the highest marginal revenue product for that land. But today there are no farms in Berkeley because industry and housing developers bought up the farms and changed the land use. As the population of Berkeley increased, the land was worth more to industry and to housing developers than it was to the farmers. So the farmers sold their land.

10. Swampy land has a high marginal revenue product for a rice farmer and a low marginal revenue product for a corn farmer. So the land will be sold to the rice farmer, who is willing to pay a higher price for the land than the corn farmer.

11. External finance means borrowing money to pay for an investment good

(machine or new building). Internal finance means using the business's own money to pay for the investment good.

12. The investment decision rule is buy the capital if the expected rate of return exceeds the interest rate, and don't buy the capital if the interest rate exceeds the expected rate of return. The rule is the same whether the investment is financed externally or internally.

13. Your brother should buy new sound equipment if he can get the money for the project for less than 8%.

14. When interest rates decline, we move along an investment demand curve to a higher level of investment spending.

15. When expected future sales decline, expected rates of return fall. If interest rates do not change, investment spending will fall.

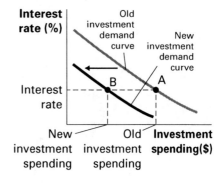

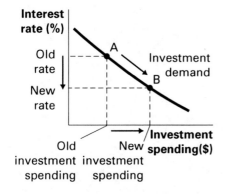

Index

CPSIA information can be obtained at www.ICGtesting.com
Printed in the USA
BVOW00n0952140813

328552BV00003B/4/P